THE RETURN OF
ANTI-SEMITISM

THE RETURN OF
ANTI-SEMITISM

Gabriel Schoenfeld

ENCOUNTER BOOKS
SAN FRANCISCO

First edition published in 2004 by Encounter Books, an activity of Encounter for Culture and Education, Inc., a nonprofit tax exempt corporation.

Encounter Books website address: www.encounterbooks.com

Manufactured in the United States and printed on acid-free paper.

The paper used in this publication meets the minimum requirements of ANSI/NISO Z39.48-1992 (R 1997)(*Permanence of Paper*).

FIRST EDITION

Library of Congress Cataloging-in-Publication Data

Schoenfeld, Gabriel.
    The return of anti-semitism / Gabriel Schoenfeld.
    p. cm.
    Includes bibliographical references and index.
    ISBN 1-893554-89-9 (alk. paper)
    1. Antisemitism—History—20th century. I. Title.
DS145.S2799 2004
305.892'4'0090511—dc22

                                                            2003064319

10   9   8   7   6   5   4   3   2   1

To Neal Kozodoy,
brilliant editor, true friend

CONTENTS

ONE

WARNING SIGNS

O ver the past several years, I have watched as ever tighter security restrictions have been set up in and around the building where I work in New York City. First came a redesign of the main entranceway to add a "man-trap," two bullet- and explosion-proof glass and steel doors that form a chamber through which all visitors must pass. Next came the installation of "Jersey barriers," heavy concrete emplacements on the sidewalk that form a perimeter through which a truck- or car-bomber cannot easily penetrate. Then the windows of the building were laminated with a special plastic designed to keep glass from shattering in a blast. An electronic "sniffing" device was placed in the lobby to screen incoming mail for explosives. Video surveillance cameras were installed on the exterior of the building, and a professional security firm with uniformed guards was hired to monitor the cameras and to inspect the personal possessions of visitors. For a period of time, the New York City Police Department assigned a patrolman to guard the building's front door.

The building is headquarters of a national Jewish organization. One block away is a large and beautiful synagogue, the oldest Jewish house of worship in continuous use in the city. This Moorish-style landmark is also now surrounded by Jersey barriers, and congregants attending services on Saturdays and holidays are guarded by the police. The same is true of a great

1

many synagogues and Jewish institutions throughout the New York area, across the United States, and around the world.

In my office building, as at my synagogue, we have rapidly grown accustomed to the new security regime; when the subject is discussed at all, our remarks are usually attended by resignation or dark mirth. In the face of terrorists willing to fly hijacked jet aircraft into skyscrapers, what genuine protection, one wonders, can heightened security actually provide? But as I have watched the building harden itself against attack, I have also felt an increasing sense of dismay and anger, even fury. As recently as five years ago, such measures would have been as unnecessary as they were inconceivable. Now they are ubiquitous. The plain fact is that something unprecedented is taking place: Jews in the United States are being targeted for murder. How did we reach this pass, and how did we come to accept it so blithely?

Such questions, and others that followed from them, provoked me to write this book, which is the story of how, virtually unnoticed and unremarked, a lethal hatred of Jews has once again come to play a large part in world events. Telling the story entailed proceeding in the same way an epidemiologist might, tracing the byways on which a pathogen has traveled from one location to another.

To anyone even modestly acquainted with current events, it is readily apparent that the Islamic world is today the epicenter of a particularly virulent brand of anti-Semitic hatred. But it is far less apparent how and why this came to be the case. Uncovering the origins of Islamic anti-Semitism, and the reasons why this quadrant of humanity has proved so eager both to consume the poison and to peddle it, is one major and absolutely crucial element of the story I wish to tell.

But the passions roiling the Islamic world are hardly the end of the matter. For anti-Semitism has also reawakened dramatically in Europe, where it was long thought to be completely dormant if not entirely extinct. And it is also making unprecedented headway in new precincts in the United States, a country where it has never before found truly fertile soil.

This reawakening has implications extending far beyond the Jewish community. In his posthumously published master-piece, *Defying Hitler,* Sebastian Haffner noted how, in 1930s Germany, the passions unleashed against the Jews were fungible: "Once the violence and readiness to kill that lies beneath the surface of human nature has been awakened and turned against other humans, and even made into a duty, it is a simple matter to change the target." [1] Haffner set those words to paper in early 1939. Only months after he did so, much of the world was in flames; along with six million Jews, tens of millions more would perish in the war that Hitler fomented.

Today, the same transpositional possibilities do not merely threaten us; they are already upon us. Those in Pakistan who beheaded the journalist Daniel Pearl as they forced him to utter the words, "my father's Jewish, my mother's Jewish, I'm Jewish," have already selected other targets for destruction in their zeal to eliminate Jews and other infidels from the face of the earth. Although our government hardly acknowledges the fact, and fails to orient its policies accordingly, the United States is now locked in a conflict with adversaries for whom hatred of Jews lies at the ideological core of their beliefs.

❖

In attempting to account for these developments, I have reached a set of conclusions about why events are unfolding as they are. Some of these conclusions are obvious and familiar; they revolve around the way certain perduring myths have time and again served to fuel suspicion and fear and hatred of Jews. But some of my conclusions are far more surprising, even counterintuitive.

One is that, today, the most vicious ideas about Jews are primarily voiced not by downtrodden and disenfranchised fringe elements of society but by its most successful, educated and "progressive" members. This is true in the Islamic world, and it is even truer in the West. One is less likely to find anti-Semites today in beer halls and trailer parks than on college campuses and among the opinion makers of the media elite.

This shift reflects an unexpected twist in the helix of anti-Semitism's DNA. In the past, anti-Semitism has typically come to the fore in undemocratic countries, and almost always in periods of great economic and political stress. But Europe today is democratic and tranquil, as is the United States, yet the disease is spreading nonetheless. This development places a crucial question squarely before us: are we witnessing a repeat performance of an old play or the beginning of something new? An answer, alas, can hardly be definitive. Anti-Semitism is a complex historical virus. And like any such organism it is composed of a variety of strains: ancient and modern, racialist and religious, left-wing and right-wing.

During the last century, we became intimately familiar with the right-wing variety, with its racialist and religious roots: the variety that found its most extreme expression in the Nazi era. Today, with that form of anti-Semitism utterly discredited, it is another tradition—anti-Semitism of the Left—that is gaining respectability and momentum. The roots of this strain can be traced back to the Enlightenment.

The eighteenth-century avatars of universal reason could not but perceive Judaism as the enemy of their rationalist faith; as the tree trunk from which the branch of Christianity had sprung, the religion of the Hebrew Bible was, they contended, ultimately responsible for Europe's subjugation to an irrational creed and the arbitrary reign of clerics. And the Enlightenment's apostles of tolerance were not exactly tolerant when it came to living Jews: a "nation of usurers," in the words of Immanuel Kant; the flag-bearers of "superstitious blindness," in the words of Baron d'Holbach. This strand of anti-Semitism, having proliferated several branches of its own—socialist, populist, liberal—is today supplanting its right-wing cousin to become the dominant form of anti-Semitism in the West. Paradoxically, because Jews are so heavily over-represented on the Left, one finds a significant contingent of Jews who are themselves promoting nakedly anti-Semitic ideas.

The future force of this emerging Western form of anti-Semitism is impossible to gauge. As an intellectual movement it is not particularly impressive. Indeed, among its leading exponents are several crackpots and cranks. But because it is becoming increasingly energetic at the same moment that Islamic anti-Semitism is flourishing, it is enjoying successes far beyond what its modest numbers and the low caliber of its thinkers would suggest. A process of symbiosis is at work, and it would be cavalier to dismiss its potential.

❖

Whatever the prospects of anti-Semitism are, the past would seem to contain an ample supply of lessons about the dangers of quiescence. In 1924, Louis Marshall, a distinguished leader of the American Jewish Committee, confidently proclaimed that there was "not the slightest likelihood that the Nazis' plan will ever be carried out to the slightest extent."[2] In 1924, that seemed like an entirely reasonable prediction. It turned out to be entirely wrong. Yet even as the 1930s unfolded and the Nazis rose to power and openly proclaimed their aim of exterminating world Jewry, many still found it impossible to look evil in the face and grasp its true objectives. Few observers comprehended the depth of Adolf Hitler's obsession with the Jewish question, or the fact that he regarded both Stalin and Roosevelt as themselves tools of the Jews, or what any of this signified for the peace of the world. Willful ignorance, indifference, and stunned disbelief fed directly into the policy of appeasement, which ended with a catastrophe of unprecedented dimensions.

At present, the world does not face another Adolf Hitler. But we inhabit a planet in which there are weapons of mass destruction, where there are terrorists working assiduously to obtain such weapons, and where many of those same terrorists openly proclaim a desire to murder Jews. To complete the circle, there are also those eager to downplay the danger, who suggest that those concerned with fighting it, or even writing about it, have become prey to irrational fears or are wrongly projecting the lessons of the twentieth century onto the more secure screen of the twenty-first.

5

Are they right? Are all those concrete emplacements and bomb-sniffing devices evidence of what one such scoffer has called "ethnic panic," and a colossal waste of money to boot? Let us review the evidence.

❖

TWO

THE ISLAMIC STRAIN

The Muslim world is the necessary starting point for our inquiry. There the ancient and modern strands of anti-Semitism have been most successfully fused today, and from there the hatred of Jews receives its main propulsion outward.

An immense historical irony arises here. If the Islamic world is today an exporter of anti-Semitism, until fairly recently it has been mostly an importer, and a relatively lax one at that. Historically, hatred of Jews flourished most luxuriantly by far in Europe, and therefore many of the contemporary Islamic notions about Jews could be traced to Europe. Of course, Islam has its own, indigenous anti-Jewish traditions, which have often been scanted or overlooked by historians. These two strands, the European and the indigenous, have now merged. They are being spread across the globe by the force of the worldwide Islamic revival and the flood of petrodollars that underwrites it.

The Muslim world is an exceedingly complex and varie-gated terrain. If we were to confine ourselves just to those countries where Muslims are in the majority, we would be con-fronting some forty-six separate lands, each with its own distinct history, politics and culture. Of these forty-six coun-tries, whose combined population approaches a billion, almost half are Arab, and are thus intertwined directly or indirectly in the longstanding Arab war against Israel. This fact lends an especially fervent character to the anti-Semitism that infects almost all of them.

But even far from Israel's shores, in Islamic countries where Jews have never had a presence or played a role, the poison has spread prolifically. Malaysia, in Southeast Asia, five thousand miles from Jerusalem, is a stunning case in point. In this country of 23 million, anti-Semitism flows from the top down. Throughout his long career in public life, Mahathir Mohamad, the country's prime minister for the last two decades, has traded in harsh invective against Jews and Israel. Well before he occupied his present high office, Mahathir was pointing to the "hook-nosed Jews" who "understand money instinctively" and who, he contended, were responsible for Malaysia's continuing economic woes.[1] As prime minister, Mahathir has built on this formula both to garner public support and to deflect criticism from himself, condemning foreign newspapers like the *Wall Street Journal* as "Jewish owned" and leveling baseless charges about "Zionist plots" aimed against his government.[2] A special target has been the international financier George Soros, who he claims is part of a sinister conspiracy to undermine the Malaysian currency.

In the international arena, Mahathir has supported every resolution against Israel in the multilateral organizations of which Malaysia is a member, and has vilified Israel and Jews in whatever forums give him a platform. All Israelis are barred from entering the country; so are third-country nationals whose passports indicate a visit to Israel. At a 1986 meeting of the Non-Aligned countries, Mahathir declared that "the Nazi oppression of Jews has taught them nothing," instead transforming Jews "into the very monsters that they condemn so roundly in their propaganda material. They have been apt pupils of the late Dr. Goebbels."[3]

Not all that far from Malaysia lies Pakistan, where 98 percent of the 140 million inhabitants are Muslim; the country's minuscule Jewish population—some two thousand members of the Bene Israel community at the time the British withdrew in 1948—is long gone, having fled abroad in the face of subsequent pogroms. But even without a Jew in sight, Pakistani anti-Semitism flourishes. Michael Kamber, a writer for the *Village Voice* who spent several months in the country in the wake of 9/11, has described a society rife with the fear and hatred of Jews.[4] Almost all of his interlocutors, for example, were convinced that four thousand Jews who worked at the World Trade Center had called in sick on the morning of 9/11 to save their own lives, having been informed about the attack in advance. Nor was that all. "To me," one Islamabad mullah explained, the attack itself "seems the design of the Jewish lobby. The Jewish lobby wants to pit Islam against Christianity."

No matter what subject was under discussion, reports Kamber, government officials would

> veer off into long diatribes about the Jews; fundamentalist religious leaders, who educate hundreds of thousands of children in the country's madrassas, spoke of little else.... Seeking out more moderate voices, I introduced myself to a religious leader from Pakistan's much persecuted Shia community. He was a gentle, educated man, the keeper of a holy shrine outside the city. After we had spent some time together and I had met his family, he asked me, "So can you explain to me, why is it that America lets the Jews run everything? They run the government, the newspapers, they turn the American people against us. Why do you let the Jews spoil things between us—we could be friends." His sentiments were gentler than most.

The local origins of such Pakistani attitudes are not difficult to uncover. They reside in an educational system that is utterly dominated by fanatical Sunni mullahs, who over the past quarter-century have constructed a dense web of madrassas. These religious academies indoctrinate impoverished Pakistani youngsters in what a leading expert on Pakistan has summarized as "a fundamentalist creed marked by obscurantism, hatred of Western civilization and of Jews, misogyny, and violent dislike of Shiite Muslims." A large number of the madrassas also provide military training to those under their tutelage. The result is a huge population of illiterate fanatics, a shapeless and easily led mass "with virtually no job skills, but thoroughly prepared for a career in extremism and jihad." Given that approximately 15 percent of the students in Pakistani madrassas are foreigners, "virtually all Islamic terrorist groups around the world have benefited from this 'educational' system."[5]

Pakistan is a desperately poor country with a per-capita GDP of approximately $2,000 per year. It could not have built such a smoothly functioning system of mass indoctrination on its own. According to the same expert, "total running costs for the madrassas in Pakistan are said…to be significantly higher than the 'federal government's budgetary allocation for education, health, family planning, etc.' The sum total is almost certainly well in excess of $1 billion a year." Where does all this money come from? Some of it is internally generated, but the lion's share flows from abroad, and especially from Saudi Arabia.

❖

Departing Asia and traveling in a westerly direction toward the Muslim Middle East, let's stop first in Iran, a country in the throes of an even more virulent anti-Semitism than Pakistan's. In fact, Iran is one of the world's major wellsprings of Judeophobia. Unlike Malaysia and Pakistan, two specimens of what has rightly been called anti-Semitism without Jews, Iran has had a sizable Jewish community dating back to ancient times. In 1979, the year in which Shah Mohammad Reza Pahlavi was swept from power, it numbered approximately 100,000, its members benefiting from a tolerance and freedom unprecedented in their millennia-long sojourn in the land. Abruptly, the Islamic revolution led by the exiled Ayatollah Ruhollah Khomeini brought this golden age to an end. Stripping away the legal equality that Iranian Jews had come to enjoy, it ushered in a steadily intensifying reign of terror. Jewish businesses became the targets of vandalism and boycotts; Jews were physically harassed and attacked on the streets.

Worse was to come. By 1999, after a decade of torment that caused the Jewish community to dwindle in numbers by three-quarters, Iranian authorities arrested thirteen Jews from the cities of Shiraz and Isfahan and placed them on trial for espionage. Among them were prominent rabbis, a shoe salesman and the owner of a textile shop. All were said to have been clandestinely communicating with Tel Aviv spymasters through the offices of a synagogue. At the trial, held after a year of detention under harsh conditions, ten of the thirteen were convicted and received long sentences. The spy ring, explained the judge helpfully in his ruling, "was founded on the basis of Judaism, and its success was due to the fact that it tried to keep religion alive."[6] Only thanks to intense outside pressure have a few of these Jews been released. In the meantime, eleven other Jews, apprehended for allegedly attempting to flee Iran, have simply vanished; Tehran refuses to account for them.

The major themes of the Iranian brand of Islamic anti-Semitism are these: alleged Jewish collusion with the deposed shah; the alleged machinations of "Zionists" who, in conjunction with Israel and the United States, are "moving the wheels" of the world economy against Iranian interests; and the alleged offenses committed by Jews centuries ago against the Prophet Muhammad, offenses that are themselves supposedly of enormous significance for understanding the nefarious conduct of Jews in the contemporary world. Iranian anti-Semitism also markets Holocaust denial: there is "no documentary evidence for the gassing of even one human being in a German camp," reported the *Tehran Times* in 2001, in a dispatch typical of hundreds.[7] Likewise in wide circulation is the *Protocols of the Elders of Zion,* the nineteenth-century czarist forgery portraying the workings of a secret cabal of Jews who gather together to plot the destiny of the world; issued by the government itself, it is available both in book and in serial form, both in Farsi and in English.

Iranian anti-Semitic propagandists make a point of erasing all distinctions among Israel, Zionism and the Jews. The state of Israel is not merely Zionist, it is also, as one Iranian publication put it, "a bunch of Jews."[8] Ridding the world of this bunch of Jews is a prime Muslim obligation: "If each one of the Muslims of the world pours a bucket of water toward

11

Israel," said the late Ayatollah Khomeini in a pronouncement repeated incessantly by today's Iranian media, "the Israelite murderers will be drowned."[9] Others are even more lurid, and more violent. In the words of one Iranian propagandist, as long as Israel "is not burned and wholly destroyed, peace and tranquility will never prevail in the region."[10] Adds Iran's Supreme Leader Ayatollah Ali Khamenei, Israel is a "cancerous tumor" that must be excised.[11]

❖

Now entering the Arab world itself, we find vitriol unrestrained. The anti-Semitic swell is by no means confined to those states still formally at war with Israel. On the contrary: Egypt, which signed a peace pact with Israel more than two decades ago, is a world leader in disseminating hatred of Jews. Nor does the intensity of anti-Semitism vary with the political character of Arab regimes. Radical secular states like Syria, Libya and Iraq may stress somewhat different themes from theocracies like Saudi Arabia, but the essential picture is the same. Neither, finally, does anti-Semitism hinge on the actual presence of a Jewish community. Though Jews have dwelled among Arabs since antiquity, today they are almost all gone, for the most part driven from their homes by terror and violence in the late 1940s and 1950s.

When the state of Israel was established in 1948, the Jews of Egypt numbered some 75,000 to 80,000 souls. Most of the Jews remaining at the time of the 1956 Suez War fled abroad in its aftermath and the persecution unleashed by Gamal Abdel Nasser; today, those still residing in Egypt number only in the hundreds. But even in the near-total absence of Jews, anti-Semitism has persisted and intensified, and now is all-pervasive.

Every conceivable theme of both ancient and modern anti-Semitism can be found in the repertoire of Egypt's haters. *Al-Akhbar* is a government-sponsored daily with a circulation approximating that of the *New York Times*. One of the newspaper's regular columnists, Fatma Abdallah Mahmoud, avers that the Jews,

> are accursed in heaven and on earth. They are accursed from the day the human race was created and from the day their mothers bore them....
>
> These accursed ones are a catastrophe for the human race. They are the virus of the generation, doomed to a life of humiliation and wretchedness until Judgment Day....
>
> Finally, they are accursed, fundamentally, because they are the plague of the generation and the bacterium of all time. Their history always was and always will be stained with treachery, falseness, and lying.[12]

In the words of another inflamed columnist, in the same newspaper, the Jews are the "most vile criminals on the face of the earth." Let us give "thanks to Hitler, of blessed memory," he writes, for taking revenge against the Jews—although Muslims "do have a complaint against him [Hitler], for his revenge on them was not enough."[13]

As this colorful piece of incitement suggests, the Holocaust is never far from the thoughts of Egypt's anti-Semites. Variations—or rather inversions—of the theme are endless. If to some, the Final Solution was not final enough, others are quite convinced it never happened at all, being nothing more than a Jewish invention, a ploy to justify Zionist aggression and extract financial payments from the innocent taxpayers of Germany and other European countries. Here again is the resourceful Fatma Abdallah Mahmoud:

> With regard to the fraud of the Holocaust...many French studies have proven that this is no more than a fabrication, a lie, and a fraud!! That is, it is a "scenario," the plot of which was carefully tailored, using several faked photos completely unconnected to the truth. Yes, it is a film, no more and no less. Hitler himself, whom they accuse of Nazism, is in my eyes no more than a modest "pupil" in the world of murder and bloodshed. He is completely innocent of the charge of frying them in the hell of his false Holocaust!!
>
> ...But I, personally and in light of this imaginary tale, complain to Hitler, even saying to him from the bottom of my heart, "If only you had done it, brother, if only it had really happened,

so that the world could sigh in relief [without] their evil and sin."[14]

Too crude? Mohamed Heikal is by any standard the dean of Egyptian journalism, the author of well-regarded histories, a number of which have appeared in English, and the former editor of the daily *Al-Ahram,* which he built into the influential newspaper that it is. Urbane, sophisticated, at ease in the capitals of Europe, Heikal is another fervent Holocaust denier. In a fawning preface to the 1998 Arabic edition of Roger Garaudy's notorious tract, *The Founding Myths of Modern Israel,* Heikal contends that the mass murder of Europe's Jews in gas chambers is a "legend" and a "myth." Indeed, he is persuaded that "the number of Jews in the world after the war of 1939–1945 was the same as it had been before the war." Rather than six million dead, Jewish victims of Nazism "did not exceed 300,000 or 400,000."

Credit for establishing these and other supposed facts belongs to historians who have been endlessly hounded and persecuted—Heikal has in mind not only Garaudy but the Holocaust denier David Irving, a "meticulous" historian who, he says, has "come the closest of all researchers to the truth" about the Final Solution and has therefore been "harassed and physically assaulted in the street."[15]

❖

If rampant Holocaust denial is one strain of Egyptian anti-Semitism, the ancient blood libel is another. "The Talmud, the second holiest book for the Jews," reports *Al-Akhbar,* "determines that the 'matzos' of Atonement Day [*sic*] must be kneaded 'with blood' from a non-Jew. The preference is for the blood of youths after raping them!!"[16]* Egypt is also a prime distributor of the *Protocols of the Elders of Zion,* which exists in at least nine different Arabic translations and has gone through

---

*Not that it matters, but matzah, unleavened bread, is eaten on Passover and not on "Atonement Day" (Yom Kippur); it is made of flour and water only.

countless editions. Lately, the Egyptian government went so far as to televise this notorious text in the form of a docudrama, *Horseman without a Horse,* bringing it into millions of households across the Middle East in prime time. "By means of this series," explains the producer and star of the show, Muhammad Sobhi, "I am exposing all the Protocols of the Elders of Zion that have been implemented to date, including those that supposedly oblige Jews to corrupt the world by engaging in pornography, prostitution, and drugs."[17] For his part, Egypt's information minister, Safwat al-Sherif, has insisted that the show contains no anti-Semitic content.

The *Protocols* is not the only forgery widely circulated in and by Egypt. "The Jews Are Bloodsuckers and Will Yet Conquer America," reports the government weekly, *Akher Sa'a,* offering in proof a facsimile of a manuscript purportedly written by none other than Benjamin Franklin. At the time of the American Constitutional Convention, it seems, the great man denounced the Jews as "vampires" and advocated their expulsion from the new country by force:

> If they are not excluded from the United States by the Constitution, within at least 100 years, they shall stream into this country in such numbers that they shall rule and destroy us and change our form of government for which we Americans shed our blood and sacrificed our lives, property, and personal freedom....
>
> If the Jews are not excluded within 200 years, our children will be working in the fields to feed the Jews while they remain in the counting houses, gleefully rubbing their hands.[18]

The document containing these predictions, *Akher Sa'a* asserts, is preserved in the collection of the Franklin Institute in Philadelphia.

Need it be pointed out that there is no such document in that archive and that Benjamin Franklin never penned these loathsome words? Rather, the fake facsimile first appeared in a collection entitled *A Handbook on the Jewish Question,* published in 1935 by a Nazi "research" institute devoted to Jewish affairs. Though the origins of the forgery are well known, at least to those who wish to know, it has surfaced time and again in the Arab world and has been vouched for by respectable sources.

Every branch of the Egyptian media, from the highly specialized to the broadly popular, disseminates similar material. The highly specialized: "Jewish tourists infected with AIDS are traveling around Asian and African countries with the aim of spreading the disease," reports *Al-'ilm,* a leading Egyptian science monthly, on whose editorial board sit ranking government educational and scientific officials.[19] The broadly popular: "I Hate Israel" is the name of a hit song that in 2001 became one of the best-selling Egyptian records of all time, with some five million copies in circulation. So wildly popular was it that rival claimants to its authorship stepped forward.[20] Whoever its creator may be, there is no disputing the resonance of its message. After all, as a senior at Cairo University explained to a Western journalist, "we [Egyptians] hate Israel and we hate Jews."[21]

❖

Fiercely though the fires of hatred burn in Egypt, and useful though the government finds those flames, Egypt is also not an entirely closed society; one can find dissenting views and even, on rare occasion, direct criticism of anti-Semitism. By contrast, Saudi Arabia is monolithic. The ruling royal family conceives of itself as a jealous guardian of the puritanical Wahhabi strain of Islam that is the official religion and is shot through with hatred of Jews. Dissident voices are rare to nonexistent.

There are no Jews on the Arabian peninsula. In the seventh century, Muhammad expelled or killed the various Jewish tribes of the south, while those remaining in the north were forced off the Hijaz later in the same century under the rule of Caliph Omar. In the far south, in what came to be called Yemen, Jews did remain until the middle of the last century, when 43,000 left for Israel in a single year in an air evacuation called "Operation Magic Carpet." By 1968, fewer than two hundred Jews remained. As for contemporary Saudi Arabia,

Jews are forbidden to enter the kingdom, although some dispensation has been made for visiting American diplomats (most famously, Henry Kissinger) and more recently for American soldiers entering the land to protect the oilfields. But whatever ambiguity exists in Saudi immigration and border restrictions, it is amply compensated for by the clarity of the media, which are an unceasing font of wild anti-Jewish vitriol.

One major outlet is *Al-Riyadh,* the leading Saudi newspaper and, like all publications in the country, under tight government rein. One gets a flavor of the paper's style from the way it has parlayed a twist on the ancient blood libel to terrify its readers. In this version, Jews are ludicrously accused of using the blood of Gentile adolescents—not, as Egypt's *Al-Akhbar* had it, to prepare matzah for the fast day of Yom Kippur, but rather to make pastry for another annual celebration, the holiday of Purim. *Al-Riyadh* fabricates as follows:

> The Jewish people must obtain human blood so that their clerics can prepare the holiday pastries. In other words, the practice cannot be carried out as required if human blood is not spilled!!
>
> ...For this holiday, the victim must be a mature adolescent who is, of course, a non-Jew—that is, a Christian or a Muslim. His blood is taken and dried into granules. The cleric blends these granules into the pastry dough; they can also be saved for the next holiday....
>
> Let us now examine how the victims' blood is spilled. For this, a needle-studded barrel is used; this is a kind of barrel, about the size of the human body, with extremely sharp needles set in it on all sides. [These needles] pierce the victim's body, from the moment he is placed in the barrel.
>
> These needles do the job, and the victim's blood drips from him very slowly. Thus, the victim suffers dreadful torment— torment that affords the Jewish vampires great delight as they carefully monitor every detail of the bloodshedding with pleasure and love that are difficult to comprehend.
>
> After this barbaric display, the Jews take the spilled blood, in the bottle set in the bottom [of the needle-studded barrel], and the Jewish cleric makes his coreligionists completely happy on

their holiday when he serves them the pastries in which human blood is mixed.

There is another way to spill the blood: The victim can be slaughtered as a sheep is slaughtered, and his blood collected in a container. Or, the victim's veins can be slit in several places, letting his blood drain from his body.[22]

And onward the fantasy rolls. In the Saudi press, royal officials and especially the theocrats who preside over the country's network of government-subsidized mosques routinely refer to Jews as the "brothers of apes and pigs." According to *Al-Jazirah,* a state-controlled daily newspaper, "Allah decreed that the Jews would be humiliated; he cursed them, and turned them into apes and pigs."[23] A long line of Islamic texts, beginning with the Qur'an, is adduced to support this contention, although it is also noted that in the ninth century a number of authorities regarded Jews as mice and lizards instead. In contemporary Saudi Arabia, children are indoctrinated with these beliefs from an early age. Here is an excerpt from an interview with a *toddler* on the government-controlled television station IQRAA:

> *Host:* What's your name?
> *Basmallah:* Basmallah.
> *Host:* Basmallah, how old are you?
> *Basmallah:* Three and a half.
> *Host:* Are you a Muslim?
> *Basmallah:* Yes.
> *Host:* Basmallah, are you familiar with the Jews?
> *Basmallah:* Yes.
> *Host:* Do you like them?
> *Basmallah:* No.
> *Host:* Why don't you like them?
> *Basmallah:* Because…
> *Host:* Because they are what?
> *Basmallah:* They're apes and pigs.
> *Host:* Because they are apes and pigs. Who said they are so?
> *Basmallah:* Our God.

Host: Where did he say this?
Basmallah: In the Qur'an.[24]

Somehow, in the view of the clerics who teach such doctrines, these "apes and pigs" magically constitute the sinister force behind almost every significant event in the world. In one recent televised discussion, an imam explained how the attack of September 11 was a "continuation of the Jewish deception and the Jewish-Zionist wickedness which infiltrates the U.S." If Americans mistakenly believed the attack was the work of Muslims, this was because the media are "in the hands of the Jews and behind it there are the despicable fingerprints of the Jewish Zionists that change reality." There is nothing these Jews will not stoop to, for they "are the most despicable people who walked the land and are the worms of the entire world."[25]

A little of this stuff goes a very long way, as we shall see. Propelled by money, organization and vision, it reaches clear around the world. But let us first complete our tour of the Arab world. As in Egypt and Saudi Arabia, a similar pattern obtains in Syria, not a theocracy but a Ba'athist "revolutionary" state. Syrian textbooks teach elementary school students about "the treacherous intention harbored in the Jews' souls," and about the "deception and conspiracy" in which they perpetually engage. High school students are given more advanced lessons about the "aggressive [and] evil tendency that is rooted in the Jewish personality," and about how the Jews "threaten Islamic and Arab existence with destruction and extinction." So dangerous are the Jews, explains one textbook, so vile are their crimes, that "the logic of genuine justice decrees against them one verdict, the carrying-out of which is unavoidable. Their criminal intention should be turned against them by way of their elimination."[26]

The perfidy of the Jews has become something of an obsession with none other than Field Marshal Mustafa Tlass, Syria's minister of defense. Tlass is the author of a book rehearsing the details of the nineteenth-century Damascus Affair in which, according to his less than fully informed version of this notorious episode, a priest "fell victim to a group of Jews who sought to drain his blood to prepare baked goods for their Yom Kippur holiday."[27] At the International Book Fair held in Syria in late 2002, Tlass's book was on display in reprint, bound together with another title, *The Young Martyr of Prague,* telling the story of a young convert to Christianity murdered at the hands of his Jewish father. The volume, according to the London-based Arab newspaper *Al-Hayat,* is "very popular" with the younger generation who want to "know about the Jews, how they harmed Arabs and others, and their motives to murder other human beings."[28]

❖

Finally, passing to the front lines, we turn to the Palestinian Arabs. Under the Oslo Accords, the Palestinians pledged to cease propagating hatred against Jews and Israelis. Instead, their murderous outpourings have been constant and unceasing. True, since Palestinian society is in a condition of flux, anti-Semitism has manifested itself there in a more complex pattern than in iron-bound regimes like Syria and Saudi Arabia, or even Egypt. Yasir Arafat himself hails from the secular Arab revolutionary tradition in which a loose brand of Marxism conjoins with pan-Arab radicalism; the result is that he speaks less of perfidious Jews than of a Zionist movement that is "racist and fanatic in its nature, aggressive, expansionist, and colonial in its aims, and fascist in its methods." But if Arafat himself has habitually cast the Palestinian-Israeli conflict in political rather than religious terms, plain old unvarnished anti-Semitism has nevertheless had its uses to him, as a look at the publications under his Palestinian Authority (PA) amply shows.

"Corruption is a Jewish trait worldwide," reports *Al-Hayat al-Jadida,* the Palestinian Authority's daily newspaper. Indeed, so prevalent is this trait

> that one can seldom find corruption that was not masterminded by Jews or that Jews are not responsible for. They are well known for their intense love of money and its accumulation.

The way in which they get hold of that money does not interest them in the least. On the contrary—they would use the most basic despicable ways to realize their aim, so long as those who might be affected were non-Jews. A Jew would cross any line if it were in his interest.[29]

The same publication, in an article entitled "Jewish Control of the World Media," expressed wonderment at the ability of the Jews "to brainwash American and European public opinion" into thinking them a "wise, courageous, ingenious, dexterous, and ambitiously innovative people?!" But then, the paper recalls, this is an old story: the Nazi era, too, proved an enormous boon to the Jews, who "concocted horrible stories of gas chambers which Hitler, they claimed, used to burn them alive," all in order to "rouse empathy and claim reparations, donations, and grants from around the world."[30]

Palestinian schools, the seedbeds of future generations' attitudes, faithfully reflect the same mindset. In flagrant violation of the Oslo Accords, textbooks and teachers' guides have ensured that an implacable hatred of the enemy is transmitted effectively to the young. "Write in your exercise book," instructs one primer, about "an event showing the fanaticism of the Jews in Palestine." Student workbooks routinely pose questions like: "Why do the Jews hate Muslim unity and want to cause division among them?" or "Give an example of the evil attempts of the Jews, from events happening today."[31] From here it is but the smallest of steps to the conclusion that any and all means are permissible—nay, praiseworthy—to eliminate this scourge from the earth.

So it is, as well, in the religious councils of the Palestinian Authority. Ikrima Sabri, the Palestinian mufti and the ranking cleric of the PA, has explained that "it is the art of the Jews to deceive the world. But they can't do it to us." Further, "all those Jews who came here from all over the world, must return to the places from where they came."[32] Sheikh Ibrahim Madhi, an Arafat-appointed imam, preaches sermons that are frankly genocidal, including remonstrations to Allah to "accept our martyrs in the highest Heaven. Oh, Allah, show the Jews a black day. Oh, Allah, annihilate the Jews and their supporters."[33] Another figure appointed by Arafat, Ahmad Abu Halabiya, has implored his brethren on Palestinian television to "Have no mercy on the Jews, no matter where they are, in any country. Fight them, wherever you are. Wherever you meet them, kill them."[34]

The secular figures in the Palestinian Authority are no better. Mahmoud Abbas, who served briefly as prime minister and whom the Associated Press characterized as "urbane," "moderate" and a "pragmatist"—and who many hoped would finally lead the Palestinians into a peace agreement with Israel—spent three years in Moscow writing a doctoral dissertation entitled "The Other Side: The Secret Relationship between Nazism and the Zionist Movement."[35] Openly following the lead of the French Holocaust denier Robert Faurisson, Abbas contended that the gas chambers and crematoria at Auschwitz and kindred camps were used only to disinfect prisoners and to dispose of the remains of those who died of natural causes.[36]*

If such are the ideas held by leading figures of the PA, what can one say of the supposedly more extreme groups like Hamas, Hizbollah and Islamic Jihad? Setting aside tactical and theoretical differences among themselves, the strain of anti-Semitism they peddle varies from that of the PA mostly in its greater frequency and intensity. *Al-Istiqlal,* the weekly newspaper of Islamic Jihad, describes Jews as "made of treachery and deceit [and] marked by perfidy and treason," as living in "a constant state of conflict and continuous aggression," and as motivated by a "pressing desire to accumulate money in order to satisfy their unrestrained passions toward evil."[37] Hassan Nasrallah, the secretary-general of Hizbollah, speaks of Jewish "acts of madness and slaughter," most notoriously in conquer-

---

*In one of its flattering portraits of Abbas, the *New York Times* (June 14, 2002) described him simply as a "historian," noting that he "holds a doctorate in history from the Moscow Oriental College." The subject of his research, the U.S. newspaper of record blandly reported, was "Zionism."

ing Palestine, where this "people without a name" engaged in "massacres, slashed open the bellies of pregnant women, slaughtered children, women, men and old people, destroyed houses, wiped out entire villages, and founded a state of their own on land stolen through acts of slaughter, terrorism, violence, and cruelty." In Nasrallah's measured view, Israel is "a cancerous body in the region.... When a cancer is discovered, it must be dealt with fearlessly; it must be uprooted."[38]

❖

One could continue presenting such material indefinitely. Not only is an inexhaustible supply of it already in circulation in the Islamic and Arab world, but every day brings fresh offerings. Nor have we tapped the rich veins provided by countries like Libya or Yemen and the small sheikhdoms of the Persian Gulf, or the radical factions of strife-torn Lebanon, or "moderate" Morocco (where three million people took to the streets in a demonstration in April 2002 chanting the slogan, "The great God is a storm that will destroy the Jews").[39] Nor have we traveled to Central Asia's Fergana Valley, a hotbed of radicalism, where the Islamic Movement of Uzbekistan (IMU), an al-Qaeda affiliate, inculcates its adepts not only with the techniques of poisons and explosives but also with hatred—not only hatred of Russians but also hatred of Jews.

The point has been established: almost wherever one turns in the Islamic world, anti-Semites have found a home, and even where they do not dominate, one will seldom find anyone either opposing or discrediting them. Where exactly does this hatred come from?

More than a decade and a half ago, the distinguished historian of the Middle East, Bernard Lewis, pondered the significance of the growing ubiquity of anti-Semitic materials in that part of the world—the "volume of...books and articles published, the size and number of editions and impressions, the eminence and authority of those who write, publish, and sponsor them, their place in school and college curricula, [and] their role in the mass media." All this, Lewis wrote, might lead one to conclude that "classical anti-Semitism is an essential part of Arab intellectual life at the present time—almost as much as happened in Nazi Germany, and considerably more than in late 19th and early 20th century France."[40]

But Lewis then proceeded to qualify this bleak appraisal. Despite the abundant presence of anti-Semitic *ideas,* largely missing from the Arab Middle East was "the kind of deep, intimate hatred characteristic of the classic anti-Semite in Central and Eastern Europe and sometimes elsewhere."[41] In accounting for this, Lewis took note of a "certain ingrained courtesy in the Arab cultural tradition," which served as a kind of restraint on the expression of personal animosity directed openly at actual living Jews.[42] He also found that Arab anti-Semitism, though widespread, was in some basic sense artificial, not a spontaneous outpouring from the street but an ideological graft imposed by elites in the service of their political ends—the primary such end being the pursuit of the conflict with Israel.

As "something that comes from above, from the leadership, rather than from below, from the society," Arab anti-Semitism, wrote Lewis, was merely "a political and polemical weapon, to be discarded if and when it is no longer required."[43] If Arab leaders were to follow the path of President Anwar Sadat of Egypt, who in 1979 had come forward to make peace with the Jewish state, and if Israelis found the wherewithal to respond in kind, then it might be "possible," Lewis speculated, "that the anti-Semitic campaign will fade away, and be confined, as in the modern West, to fringe groups and fringe regimes."[44]

Lewis's analysis may have been accurate in the year in which it appeared. But from our present vantage point, it appears unduly sanguine, and at least one element has been flatly contradicted by events. In Jordan and Egypt, the anti-Semitic flood has not abated in the years since peace accords with Israel were signed; on the contrary, in both countries the vilification has swelled. Even more significant are developments in the nascent Palestinian state on the West Bank and in Gaza.

As I have already suggested, the agreements between the Palestinian Liberation Organization and Israel, first signed in 1993 and amended in 1995, called on both sides to "abstain from incitement, including hostile propaganda, against each other" and to institute "legal measures to prevent such incitement by any organizations, groups, or individuals within their jurisdiction."[45] Instead of subsiding with the arrival of "peace," however, the abuse aimed by official Palestinian sources at Jews and Israelis alike became more prevalent and more deafening. Such anti-Semitism may come "from above, from the leadership," as Lewis wrote, and it may be a "political and polemical weapon." But clearly it is also something that has diffused broadly within Palestinian Arab society and culture, assuming a genuine measure of spontaneity, to the extent that one wonders whether it could indeed be "discarded" on command.

❖

How did so many tens of millions of Arabs and Muslims become infected with so pathological, so patently irrational a creed? Several lines of analysis have been devoted to answering this question; they are not exclusive but mutually reinforcing.

One obvious starting place, suggested by the anti-Semitic earthquakes of Christian Europe, is that xenophobic hatred of one kind or another tends to come to the fore in situations of crisis or war or both. In particular, no developed country has purchased the accoutrements of modernity, of industrialization and sustained economic growth, without paying a stiff price in social and economic dislocation. In the case of Germany and Russia, the down payment in human suffering and loss of life proved to be staggering, and in both countries it involved widespread hatred of Jews.

In the Arab world, anti-Semitism has reached a decibel level well exceeding the USSR's and equaling that of Nazi Germany at its peak; but the Arab countries occupy their own peculiar segment on the arc of development. They have embarked on the transition to modernity, but their progress has been tortuously slow and startlingly unbalanced, with certain features emerging notably stunted and others grotesquely warped. A remarkable portrait of this overall condition can be found in the *Arab Human Development Report 2002,* a document produced under the auspices of the United Nations by a group of Arab social scientists.[46] A curious mixture of euphemism and candor, it sheds considerable light on how and why a pathogen like anti-Semitism could have proliferated so widely.

The report begins by commending the progress made by Arab countries in recent decades—an emollient note designed to smooth the reception of the sensitive material that follows. For the study as a whole, compiling social indicators from all twenty-two Arab countries, presents a picture of a region mired in desolation and backwardness, and, thanks to entrenched political and cultural characteristics, falling further and further behind the rest of the world.

Basic macroeconomic statistics offer a crude introduction to the region's profound underlying problems. In 1999, gross domestic product (GDP) for all the Arab countries combined stood at $531 billion. That number is smaller than the GDP of a *single* European country like Spain, whose population is one-seventh of the total Arab pool of 280 million. When one considers that a large fraction of the combined Arab GDP is derived not from services or industrial and agricultural production but from the extraction of oil and natural gas, the extent of economic underdevelopment becomes even more staggering to contemplate.

The human consequences are reflected in the rates of both unemployment and poverty. For decades, average unemployment in the Arab countries has remained static at approximately 15 percent, one of the highest rates for any region in the world. Incomes are likewise on the bottom end of the global scale, with one out of every five persons subsisting on less than $2 a day. Such destitution, the report stresses, is only part of a far broader "nexus of poverty" ranging from "poor or unavailable health care" to a "degraded habitat" and "scant or non-existent social-safety nets."[47]

It gets worse. The Arab educational system is on the

whole dysfunctional. One direct consequence of this is that illiteracy is rampant and rising, with approximately 65 million adult Arabs unable to read or write. The condition of Arab intellectual life is particularly dismal. The average output of scientific papers stands at approximately 2 percent of that of an industrialized country; citations of Arab publications by other scientists are infinitesimal; and the number of patents granted—a measure of the rate at which science moves into the economy—is negligible.

The same deficiencies that cripple science are reflected in culture, where the shortcomings are perhaps most startling of all. A condition taken for granted by citizens of the West is openness: borders are highly permeable to information; books and articles from other countries and languages are easily accessible for purchase and widely available in translation. These essential prerequisites for the production and dissemination of knowledge are virtually absent in the Arab world. The number of foreign-language books translated into Arabic annually stands at an astonishing one-fifth of the number translated in a single small European country like Greece. At the same time, the report finds a "severe shortage of writing" done in Arab countries, with a large portion of what *is* done consisting of "religious books and educational publications" that, it is laconically noted, are "limited in their creative content."[48]

A broken educational system is one symptom of backwardness. Deeper causes, the *Arab Human Development Report* suggests, include a "lack of genuine representative democracy" and a concomitant "freedom deficit."[49] Arab governments rest on "obsolete norms of legitimacy," consist largely of "a powerful executive branch that exerts significant control over all other branches of the state," and dominate the societies beneath them, untrammeled by "institutional checks and balances."[50] Forgone under this kind of authoritarian rule are the liberties—of expression, of association—so essential for a vigorous civil society.

❖

The *Arab Human Development Report 2000,* as I have noted, is a ruthlessly candid document, stating truths about the Arab world that are seldom voiced by Arabs themselves. It is also a product of the Arab milieu; had it not been supervised by the cautious bureaucrats of the United Nations and authored by Arab social scientists, it almost certainly would have painted an even starker and more alarming picture. More significantly, it would not have stooped to one ritualistic gesture that reflects all too well the same set of ailments that the scholars purport to be combating, ailments that in this case reach into the most educated and reform-minded sectors of Arab opinion.

What I have in mind is this: Having scathingly explained the internal factors of Arab society that retard its development, having further suggested that entrenched Arab xenophobia is "at odds with...the globalizing world," and having stressed that Arab societies need to instill a respect for differences that extends "beyond mere tolerance and incorporate[s] a positive attitude to other people," the report turns around and traces the arrested condition of Arab development to...the state of Israel.[51] Israel's occupation of Arab lands, it maintains, is "one of the most pervasive obstacles to security and progress," harming "nearly all aspects of human development and human security, directly for millions and indirectly for others."[52] Far from imposing suffering on Palestinians alone, Israel's behavior "casts a pall across the political and economic life of the entire region."[53]

This is rich: tiny Israel, with a population of six million and an area of 8,000 square miles, exercises such extraordinary and nefarious influence over all the vast Arab lands that, everywhere one looks, it "freezes growth, prosperity, and freedom."[54] In actual fact, by any gauge of economic and social welfare, the status of Palestinian Arabs improved far more rapidly and dramatically *under Israeli governance* in the two and a half decades before Oslo than did any other portion of the Arab world in the same period.[55] At the same time, to blame Israel for poverty and other social ailments in fabulously wealthy Saudi Arabia or in faraway Sudan is simply preposterous.

The schizophrenia of the report is in itself immensely revealing, though—revealing especially of the role that anti-Semitism and anti-Zionism play in the stultifying political universe of the Arab peoples. Hatred of Jews and demonization of Israel serve as a pressure-release valve from a disordered and futureless environment. And how necessary a release this is. The fact that within the span of a mere half-century, a relatively small population of Jews was able to build a flourishing industrial and agricultural economy on land that was formerly sand and swamp stands as a perpetual reproach to Arab pride. Per-capita income in Israel is $19,000, compared with a combined Arab average of $5,000. Life expectancy at birth is 77 years in Israel, compared with 66 among Arabs. Such facts alone give Arab governments a powerful incentive to demonize Israel and to hawk anti-Semitic ideas, as a way of shielding from sight their culpability for the socioeconomic morass they have fashioned with their own hands.

But Israel's economic success is hardly the only standing rebuke posed by the Jewish state to Arab regimes. The fact that Israel is a self-governing republic is far more menacing to Arab ruling elites, keenly aware that should the democratic idea spread to their own authoritarian societies, it would sweep them away along with their self-serving powers and privileges. Finally, the modern character of Israeli life produces its own powerful reaction in the tradition-bound Arab world, not only among elites but among the masses as well.

As historians of the mid-twentieth-century calamities of fascism and Nazism have long observed, the economic transformation of Central Europe pushed millions of peasants out of traditional village life into fragmented, socially isolated cities, producing a profound cultural alienation that in turn nourished extreme nationalism and anti-Semitism. *Mutatis mutandis,* this process is under way in painfully slow motion in the Middle East. "For the last several centuries," write the Iranian historians Ladan and Roya Boroumand,

> the Islamic world has been undergoing a traumatizing encounter with the West. Since this encounter began, our history

29

has been a story of irreversible modernization, but also of utter domination on the one side, and humiliation and resentment on the other. To Muslim minds the West and its ways have become a powerful myth—evil, impenetrable, and incomprehensible.[56]

The state of Israel—right next door, as it were—is perceived as a quintessential avatar of the "West and its ways." Even apart from the demonic pictures of Jews, the vision of Israeli life presented to the Arab world via official and unofficial media cannot but suggest that Israeli society, with its egalitarianism in sexual and other matters, its freewheeling and often irreverent culture, is the dreaded terminus to which the world's continuing social transformation is headed. If the Jew in a modernizing Europe became, in the words of one historian, "the symbol of modernization and modern society, and was hated as such," in the modernizing Arab world the state of Israel plays an equivalent role.[57]

❖

That the Jews of Israel are productive is irritant enough; that they are free and modern is intolerable. But the picture is darkened still further by the outcomes of successive encounters between Jews and Arabs in the harshest competitive arena of all, the battlefield. The war of 1948, Israel's war of independence, set the stage for all those that followed. On its eve, Arab leaders, under the spell of their own propaganda, had deluded themselves about the relative strengths of the two sides. The president of Syria reportedly said to a visitor, "I am happy to tell you that our army and its equipment are of the highest order and well able to deal with a few Jews."[58] In Baghdad, the Iraqi prime minister blithely explained that "all that was needed was 'a few brooms' to drive the Jews into the sea."[59]

As is well known, matters proved not so simple. The combined forces of Egypt, Iraq, Syria and Jordan suffered what came to be called the *nakhba*—the catastrophe—at the hands of a less well armed and numerically inferior adversary.

Those Arabs with a sense of realism allotted blame to defects in the organization of the Arab world, or to the

30

deficiencies of Arab armies. Others, unable to grapple with the real lessons of the conflagration, sought external explanations, grounded not in fact but in fantasy. Nasser, who came to power in Egypt by toppling a monarchy discredited by "the great defeat," decided that "it was not Israel that fought in that battle, but the imperialists." In the popular imagination, the literature of anti-Semitism served as a wellspring from which to draw conclusions about the "Satanic" nature of the Zionist victories. Wicked unseen forces were the only conceivable explanation for such an inexplicable outcome, in which the noble and courageous Arabs were defeated by those whom the Qur'an itself taught were "inferior and wretched" and who by rights deserved to live only at the sufferance of Muslim rulers.

Subsequent wars, in which Israel's superior morale was married to technological prowess, ended with Arab armies routed in stunning displays of modern warfare, inducing an enduring sense of degradation. In the June 1967 war, a meticulously planned Israeli strike destroyed the entire Egyptian air force on the ground. So paralyzed were Egyptian commanders, and so fearful of the personal consequences of their failure, that they falsely reported to Nasser that the *Israeli* air force had been wiped out, and that Israeli air bases were in the process of being obliterated. As the true scope of the disaster became clear, once again the excuse factory swung into operation: "British bombers, taking off in endless waves from Cyprus, are aiding and supplying the Israelis," Radio Damascus spuriously reported. [60]

The Yom Kippur War of October 1973, in which Egypt, exploiting the advantage of surprise, was able temporarily to seize some territory and to inflict heavy casualties on Israel, went some distance toward healing the wound. But whatever consolation the Arab world derived from it was diminished a decade later by an aerial battle over Lebanon—one of the most dramatic military engagements of the late twentieth century—in which Israel shot down ninety-two Syrian MiGs while incurring only one loss of its own. The repetitive pattern of such lopsided battles has served only to enhance the Arab sense of humiliation and to foster what the unfailingly astute commentator Fouad Ajami has called the Arab "worldview of victimology and rage."[61]

❖

While the state of Israel has clearly been a thorn tearing at the Arab side, the matter hardly rests there. The roots of Arab and Muslim anti-Semitism long antedate the conflict between Arabs and Zionists—just as they antedate the peculiar situation of cultural and material backwardness that plagues the Arab Middle East today.

Is one of these roots the great monotheistic religion of Islam? The question is not susceptible of an easy answer. Without a doubt, Islam does contain the theological seeds of anti-Semitism; but Islamic anti-Semitism, at least in its pre-modern form, is hardly equivalent to the virulent brand of demonization that until quite recently was such a pronounced feature of Christianity. True, too, Islam like Christianity is a supersessionist faith: in the Qur'an's telling of the divine past, the teachings of the Prophet Muhammad supplant those of the "peoples of the book," i.e., the parent religions of Judaism and Christianity, just as in Christianity's representation of itself, the religion of Jesus supplants Judaism. But if Islam and Christianity share a virtually inbred resentment of Judaism, there is also a critical divergence in their primordial stories; in both the Islamic and the Christian narratives, the Jews play an evil role, but the nature and the degree of evil imputed to them differs immensely.

After being rebuffed by the Jews of Medina following his arrival there in the year 622, the Prophet Muhammad successfully conquered the city, expelling or massacring the recalcitrant Jewish tribes. This seminal clash laid what the historian Ronald L. Nettler has called "a foundation of continuing theological antipathy," on which Islam would subsequently erect "an indelibly fixed notion of the Jews as a great enemy of the Muslims and their god, Allah." The image of the Jews as "arrogant renouncers" was set for centuries to come.[62] But—

and this was decisive—the clash between the two religions ended with Muslims in an unequivocally ascendant position; history had confirmed to them the superiority of their creed. Thus, in Nettler's summary,

> the constant reiteration of Jewish odiousness [in Islamic sources] was casual and descriptive rather than emotionally hateful, because Islam ruled and the Jews were in their proper place. All was politically right in Allah's world. His chosen People had come, seen, and conquered. This necessary condition for order in the universe prevailed. Islam was securely fixed in its proper role of superiority and leadership. The Jews firmly fixed in their assigned place were one of the signs of this political millennium. Their predilection for harming Islam was now contained and controlled. Hating them would have been superfluous—nay, even perhaps a sign of Muslim shakiness.[63]

How different this was from the early Christian encounter with the Jews. Instead of immediate Christian ascendancy there was a period of centuries during which the two religions were in direct competition for adherents. But the allure of Judaism was also far more than a mere institutional danger to the Christian flock. The root of the long animosity lay elsewhere, at the doctrinal heart of the Christian faith. If, in the Islamic historical narrative, the Jews were a maleficent people who resisted, fought and attempted to subvert the message of Muhammad, these transgressions pale next to the charge leveled against them in the Christian narrative. For here the Son of God Himself, part of the divinity, endures torture and death at Jewish instigation and with Jewish complicity. The crucifixion of Jesus turns the Jews, in Christian eyes, into an eternally marked people: murderers of God.

It is interesting to compare the Muslim telling of this same fateful episode. According to the Islamic holy texts, Jesus was not the Messiah at all but only one of his messengers. The Jews attempted to kill this messenger, but they were unsuccessful, nailing only his likeness or his double to a cross. They did not murder the Christian divinity, and of course they also did not murder the Prophet of Islam.

And so, although one can find the most horrendous violence inflicted on Jews by Muslims in the early period, one does
not find this violence developed into or justified by a central
theological construct. An anti-Judaic strain is embedded in the
foundational story of Islam; it is reflected in the Qur'an and in
post-Qur'anic literature; it is periodically manifest in Muslim
behavior. But until fairly recently it lacked the personal obses-
siveness, the unrestrained hatred and the terrified fears that
from the very beginning were so often in evidence in its Christian counterpart. There is nothing in early Muslim writings
akin, say, to the indictment leveled at the Jews by the fourth-
century Church Father Gregory of Nyssa:

> Murderers of the Lord, assassins of the prophets, rebels and
> detesters of God, they outrage the Law, resist grace, repudiate
> the faith of their fathers. Companions of the devil, race of
> vipers, informers, calumniators, darkeners of the mind, phari-
> saic leaven, Sanhedrin of demons, accursed, detested,
> lapidators, enemies of all that is beautiful.[64]

But we also have to qualify. The absence of such obloquy
in the early Islamic sources should hardly be taken to mean that
Islam presents an image of the Jews or of Judaism that is favor-
able in any way. Among modern historians, there has been at
some junctures a pronounced tendency to romanticize the relationship between Muslim and Jew, to dwell on the affinities
between the two faiths, to stress Muslim tolerance especially
during certain purportedly "golden" ages like medieval Spain,
even to suggest that Jews enjoyed equality in Islamic society.
This overly benignant view has rightly been discredited. The
status of Jews under Muslim rule and under the institutional
yoke of the *dhimmi* system (which "protected" Christians and
Jews as fellow peoples of the book) was perpetually subordinate. It also fluctuated widely, from periods of relative openness and considerable opportunity to periods of stark cruelty
and oppression.

❖

As a rule, however, Bernard Lewis is surely correct that even at its nadirs, the relationship between the two peoples was for the most part what he has characterized as "normal"—that is, to the extent that there was friction and persecution, it arose out of "genuine differences and specific circumstances" and not out of an overarching conception about the intrinsic malignity of the Jews.[65] "Most of the characteristic and distinctive features of Christian anti-Semitism were absent" in traditional Muslim society, writes Lewis. "There were no fears of Jewish conspiracy and domination, no charges of diabolic evil."[66] In this connection, it is significant that when, centuries after the Islamic heyday had passed, a virulent anti-Semitic strain did begin to develop in the Islamic world, it was not of native inspiration but of Christian derivation and almost wholly a European import.

Take the blood libel, which among the contemporary accusations hurled at Jews by Arabs has undoubtedly enjoyed the longest half-life. Only when the Turks acquired Constantinople in the fifteenth century did this particular slander first gain currency among adherents of Islam. It was disseminated by the Ottoman Empire's new Greek subjects, who were in turn drawing on legends circulating widely in Christian Europe. Even so, no fundamental shift occurred in the character of Muslim-Jewish relations until the late eighteenth or early nineteenth century. As the Ottoman Empire began to shudder and quake, its non-Muslim minorities came increasingly to be perceived as a subversive internal menace. In the case of the Jews, the entrance corridor for "abnormal" anti-Semitism was once again Christianity, now injecting venom via missionaries and native Christian minority groups like the Maronites and the Copts.

Through these channels, a whole series of new blood-libel cases commenced, entailing charges that Jews were murdering Muslim children (or Christian children in Muslim societies) for ritual purposes. The most notorious of these was the Damascus Affair of 1840, which we have already encountered through the literary imagination of Syria's defense minister, Mustafa Tlass. Nearly every one of these cases was set in motion not by

Muslims but by Christians, with France playing a singularly important role as an exporter of Judeophobia. In the Damascus Affair it was two French diplomats in Syria who enthusiastically promoted the fraudulent accusation that Syria's Jews were behind the disappearance of a Capuchin monk, while France's head of state, Adolph Thiers, insinuated that France's own Jews, who had been vigorously defending their Syrian brethren, were guilty of treachery.

A variety of French anti-Semitic tracts and forgeries made their way into circulation in the Islamic world around this period. They bore titles like *Corner Mysteries or the Secrets of the Jews Unmasked* and were translated into Arabic primarily by Eastern Christians.[67] However prevalent such material became, it still did not congeal into an orthodoxy. Indeed, as the Dreyfus case roiled France in the late 1890s, some sectors of the Arab press took the side of the accused Jewish captain against his French tormentors, pointing to Dreyfus's plight to illustrate the hypocrisy of culturally and politically "superior" Europe.

Nevertheless, by the late nineteenth century, as the crisis of the Ottoman Empire deepened, the tide of European anti-Semitism began to wash over an audience ever more sympathetic to it. In addition to the now more widely distributed blood libel, a new theme emerged, already richly developed in Europe. Lurid titles like *The Talmudic Human Sacrifices* began to appear, detailing the nefarious teachings allegedly contained in the sacred texts of the Jews. In the early twentieth century, one also starts to find discussions in the Arab press of the *Protocols of the Elders of Zion;* the first full translation of this forgery into Arabic, again from the French, was issued in 1926 in a periodical published by the Latin Catholic community.[68] A Christian Arab brought out the text in Cairo in book form the following year.

Then came the 1930s, a time of rising racialist fevers in Europe—and a time, too, of rising friction between Zionist settlers in Palestine and a hostile, resistant Arab world. The Nazis lost no love on Arabs, another species of *Untermenschen* in the

Nazi cosmology. Nevertheless, Nazi teachings found receptive ears among Arabs facing what they regarded as a "British-Jewish" plot to seize their territory. A variety of political parties and movements sprang up in countries across the region that emulated the Nazi system and Nazi symbols, organizing themselves in strictly hierarchical fashion and embracing the nationalist and anti-Semitic tenets of Hitlerism. They included the National Socialist Party in Lebanon and Syria, the Futuwwa in Iraq, the Young Egypt Society (also known as the "Green Shirts") and the Muslim Brotherhood in Egypt. Viciously anti-Semitic Nazi texts like Alfred Rosenberg's *The Myth of the Twentieth Century* enjoyed a broad readership, along with Hitler's *Mein Kampf,* the first Arabic edition of which was published in 1938.

By the end of World War II, the Nazi sympathizers had left a decided mark on the Arab world, and not least on the next generation of Arab leadership. Haj Muhammed Amin al-Husseini, the grand mufti of Jerusalem, the leader of the Palestinian Arabs in the war years, is one prominent figure whose influence spanned the era. An avid Nazi supporter and admirer of Hitler, he traveled to Germany in 1941 and was granted audiences with the Führer, who assured him that the Reich's war against the Jews was unrelenting. Spending the remainder of the war in Germany, the mufti participated in a broad range of activities on behalf of the Nazi war machine, personally collaborating (through a friendship with Heinrich Himmler) in the bureaucratic apparatus at work on the extermination of European Jewry. He also made occasional broadcasts on German radio to Arabic-speaking countries, augmenting Nazi propaganda with a religious twist: "Kill Jews wherever you find them, for the love of God, history, and religion."[69]

Nazism, of course, perished on the battlefield, and almost overnight its influence dwindled to nothing everywhere—everywhere, that is, but in the Arab countries. There it lived on in various guises. In the immediate postwar era, which in 1948 saw the founding of the state of Israel and the armed attempt to strangle it at birth, the Arab world was led by a cohort of men who had been thoroughly steeped in Nazi teachings. The grand mufti, in exile in Cairo and respected across the Arab world, continued to embrace the Nazi ideological package (even as he would also, in later years, attempt to forge ties with Yasir Arafat's Palestinian Liberation Organization). In Egypt, both Gamal Abdel Nasser and Anwar Sadat, two army officers who would rise successively to the top of the heap, at one point openly professed admiration for Hitler and his works. Major Arab countries, including Egypt, Syria and Iraq, became way stations and refuges for notorious German war criminals seeking to escape from justice in Europe. No sooner did the Allied forces withdraw from the region after 1945 than vicious pogroms erupted, instigated from on high and directed against the remaining Jewish communities in Iraq, Syria, Egypt, Libya and Yemen. Of the Arab leaders who came to the fore in the postwar era, only Sadat would later—famously—come to have misgivings.

By then, to be sure, a fascinating metamorphosis had taken place in world politics. The Soviet Union, Nazi Germany's bitter enemy and ideological antipode in World War II, had become, over the course of the Cold War, a major patron of the Arabs. But perhaps it was not such a metamorphosis after all—at least from the Arab point of view. Considering the intense anti-Semitism emanating from the USSR in the late Stalin era, culminating in the Doctors' Plot of 1953 and then continuing in the Khrushchev and Brezhnev eras, the alliance with the Soviet Union made perfect sense. Only the lexicon had to shift, with a left-wing rhetoric partially supplanting the out-of-date Nazi phraseology. In the Arab press, and in harmony with the teachings of *Izvestia* and *Pravda,* Israel was now depicted as an outpost of American "imperialism," and Zionism as a "racist" doctrine. The older catchwords by no means disappeared; they merely joined a somewhat dissonant chorus.

Identifying the specific tunes in this chorus can be an exercise in confusion. While Syria, for example, was an ally of Moscow, its dictator, Hafez al-Assad, would declaim from the songbook of Soviet propaganda against a Zionism that "follows a futile and obsolete ideology based on expansion, the building of settlements, and the uprooting of Arabs from land in which they had lived for centuries."[70] After the USSR disappeared, a new motif of pure Islamic provenance crept into Assad's rhetoric as he began to speak of the necessity of a "holy war" against the Jewish state. After his death in 2000, his son and successor, Bashar Assad, shifted yet again. Greeting Pope John Paul II on a visit to Damascus in 2001, the young dictator resorted to an obsolete tenet of the Catholic faith, one discarded by the Vatican itself, informing the visiting pontiff that contemporary Jews were attempting "to kill the principles of all religions with the same mentality in which they betrayed Jesus Christ."[71]*

❖

Here we touch on a matter of great moment in the development of modern Islamic anti-Semitism. At the very same time that a quasi-Marxist anti-Zionism was gaining steam under Soviet tutelage, so too was a purely *religious* brand of anti-Semitism, of a fervor and vehemence new to the Arab-Muslim world. It was part and parcel of the sweeping movement of Islamic fundamentalism, also known as Islamism, that in the last decades has transformed the face of Islam, assuming political power in some of the major countries of the Middle East and wielding enormous influence in those countries where it is not enthroned. It has found its most violent expression in the Islamic terrorist groups, ranging from Hamas to Islamic Jihad to Hizbollah to al-Qaeda.

Far less well known in the West than figures like Arafat or Nasser or Assad is Sayyid Qutb (1906–1966), perhaps the leading theoretician of Islamic fundamentalism. Yet Qutb's Arab

---

*Yasir Arafat is another Arab leader who forged a close relationship with the Kremlin and voiced its anti-imperialist slogans even as he simultaneously claimed kinship with the mufti, declaring himself proud to follow in the footsteps of this Nazi collaborator and Bolshevik enemy.

biographer is undoubtedly correct to call him "the most famous personality of the Muslim world in the second half of the 20th century," and one whose work would profoundly shape the world we live in.[72] Part of that achievement would consist in resurrecting and fashioning anew a genuinely Islamic anti-Semitism that draws from and meshes seamlessly with its Christian and Nazi cousins, while enjoying the additional authority of being firmly anchored in widely available and universally accepted Islamic sources.

To grasp Qutb's contribution, one must take note of the fact that Islam is a historical/political creed in a way that Judaism and Christianity are not. Muhammad was not only the founder of a faith but also the ruler of a dominion. From its very inception, Islam could point to its astounding earthly success as vindication of its divine teachings: at its zenith in the thirteenth century, the territory under its sovereignty extended from Africa to Asia. By the middle of the twentieth century, however, Islam's worldly standing had plummeted to unprecedented depths. Having once led the world in cultural, scientific and military accomplishment, it now lagged far behind in every realm. Its peoples had been conquered and colonized, and even Jerusalem, the holiest site in Islam after Mecca and Medina, had become the capital of a new Jewish state established with the backing of the Western powers.

Accounting for this precipitous fall from favor and finding a path to restore the Islamic world to its proper station became Qutb's main project. Born in a northern Egyptian village, the young Qutb had worked first as a teacher of Arabic and English before obtaining a sinecure in the Egyptian educational bureaucracy. He then embarked on a career as a writer and critic, winning a broad audience among Egypt's elite. A short spell in the United States from 1949 to 1951 engendered a profound revulsion at what he took to be the complete moral corruption of a country "hollow and full of contradictions, defects and evils."[73] Later he wrote: "It is astonishing to realize how primitive the American really is in his views on life. His behavior reminds us of the era of the caveman. He is primitive

40

in the way he lusts after power, ignoring ideals and manners and principles."[74]

Qutb returned to Egypt a convinced Islamic revolutionary. Arrested in 1954 for his activities in the Muslim Brotherhood, he spent the next decade in an Egyptian prison. Not long after his release in 1964, he was rearrested on charges of sedition and terrorism and sentenced to death. He was executed in 1966.

Qutb's most important writings were reissued in Saudi Arabia in 1970. In "Our Struggle with the Jews," an essay from the early 1950s that helped to secure his reputation, he squarely faces the modern crisis of Islam, and no less squarely identifies the responsible agent. To Qutb, Islam's decrepitude clearly evidences how far Muslims have strayed from the historical pattern set by Muhammad: "The Muslim community," he writes in opening, "continues to suffer from the same Jewish machinations and double-dealing which discomfited the early Muslims." Jewish "wickedness," "deception" and "plotting" are what keep the Muslim world in a state of estrangement from the teachings of the Qur'an, thereby depriving it of the real sources of knowledge and power. In this diabolical purpose, the Jews proceed not only by "sword and lance" but more subtly by filling Muslim "minds with doubt and...confusion." Their real aim is to destroy Islam itself. Indeed, there is no other human group

> whose history reveals the sort of mercilessness, [moral] shirking and ungratefulness for Divine Guidance as does this one.... The Jews perpetrated the worst sort of disobedience [against Allah], behaving in the most disgustingly aggressive manner and sinning in the ugliest way. Everywhere the Jews have been they have committed unprecedented abominations.
>
> From such creatures who kill, massacre and defame prophets one can only expect the spilling of human blood and any dirty means which would further their machinations and evilness.[75]

A key element in Qutb's analysis is that many of his fellow Muslims, particularly those occupying the seats of political and intellectual power in the Arab world, are themselves covert allies of the Jews, who "have instilled men and regimes [in the Islamic world] in order to conspire against this [Muslim] community."[76] This anti-Islamic force consists of "a massive army of agents in the form of professors, philosophers, doctors and researchers—sometimes also writers, poets, scientists and journalists."[77] In short, it was the entire advance contingent of modernity whose corrupt fruits Qutb had seen during his sojourn in the United States.

How best to combat this malign force? Qutb's answer is twofold. One must begin with a return to true Islam, which means rejecting the false creed propagated by Muslims who have fallen under the sway of Jewish deception and wickedness. From this tenet, radical Islamists across the Middle East have found inspiration for the war they have been waging against secular or insufficiently Islamic regimes. When Anwar Sadat was assassinated in 1981, not long after he had signed the Camp David Accords with Israel, his assailants were members of Egyptian Islamic Jihad, an offshoot of the Muslim Brotherhood whose leading acolytes were all admirers and disciples of Qutb.

A second component of Qutb's remedy is to go on the offensive against the Jews. Contemporary champions of Islam must recognize that their religion is facing a "Crusader-Zionist war" that demands action far beyond the mere "subjugation" of their Jewish enemies.[78] Subjugation would allow the Jews to continue fighting "through conspiracies, treacheries, and activating their agents in evil-doing."[79] What is required instead is complete and utter vanquishment. In Muhammad's time, this had been accomplished by expelling the Jews from the entire Arabian peninsula and, in gruesomely efficient fashion, killing those who remained.* In the modern era, Qutb points out,

---

*The methods employed have modern echoes. As we learn from a standard biography of Muhammad, for example, the Jewish men and women of the Banū Quraiza tribe "were penned up for the night in separated yards.... [They] spent the night in prayer, repeating passages from their scriptures, and exhorting one another in constancy. During the night graves or trenches...were dug in the market-place...when

"Allah brought Hitler to rule over them." Now that they are continuing in their innate evil ways, Muslims must "let Allah bring down upon the Jews people who will mete out to them the worst kind of punishment, as a confirmation of His unequivocal promise."[80]

❖

Is Sayyid Qutb's fanatical anti-Semitism representative? Is it "authentic"? The basic texts of Islam are so vast, diffuse and open to divergent readings that a multitude of branches and schools have emerged. Nevertheless, just as such mutually opposed twentieth-century doctrines as democratic socialism and Stalinism were founded upon entirely plausible readings of the nineteenth-century teachings of Karl Marx, so are the doctrines of Qutb and his fellow Islamists a plausible interpretation of Islam's sacred books. As for what percentage of the Islamic world subscribes to this particular school of thought, that is difficult to estimate, but in a world with a billion Muslims, even a small percentage means a large number.

Whatever the tally, we know from the recent history of the Middle East that the fundamentalists have gained influence and power far beyond their numbers. In Iran, a revolution was carried out under their banner; Ayatollah Khomeini was himself a disciple of Sayyid Qutb's teaching, adapting the Sunni Egyptian's theorizing to his own Shiite creed. He emphasized the "apostasy" of secularizing Muslims and strove successfully to create a state organized according to the norms and precepts of an idealized bygone age. "Since its inception," proclaimed Khomeini, "Islam was afflicted with the Jews who distorted the reputation of Islam by assaulting and slandering it, and this has continued to our present day."[81]

---

these were ready in the morning, Mahomet, himself a spectator of the tragedy, gave command that the captives should be brought forth in companies of five and six at a time. Each company was made to sit down by the brink of the trench destined for its grave, and there beheaded. Party after party they were thus led out, and butchered in cold blood, till the whole were slain." Sir William Muir, *The Life of Mahomet* (London, 1861), vol. 3, pp. 276–79.

And here is a terrible paradox. In Syria, in Egypt, even in rigidly orthodox Saudi Arabia, fundamentalists have been at odds with the established regimes, which have struggled to suppress them by various means. Yet no matter which side the contestants occupy, they tend to agree on one point: hatred of Jews and of Israel. It is the single item on which even the most determined religious extremists can find common ground with the most dedicated secularists.

The consequences of this convergence are dramatic, extending outward in concentric circles from the Middle East. The tightest ring is Israel's conflict with its immediate Arab neighbors. But for the fundamentalists, Israel's "occupation" of Palestinian lands is hardly the predominant issue. The real issue has been straightforwardly put by Hassan Nasrallah of Hizbollah. Anyone who reads the Qur'an, he says, "cannot think of co-existence with [the Jews], of peace with them, or about accepting their presence, not only in Palestine of 1948 but even in a small village in Palestine, because they are a cancer which is liable to spread again at any moment."[82]

Do Yasir Arafat's secularists disagree? Not really. In the summer of 2000, even the most far-reaching Israeli concessions, including the allocation of 97 percent of the territories captured in 1967 to the Palestinian Authority and the re-division of Jerusalem, were insufficient to assuage the PA's appetite. The result was not a counteroffer but the initiation of the second "intifada," a war that continues to the present day.

Such is the climate wrought by the perpetual incitement against Israel's very existence that even if Arafat had wished to agree to the unprecedented offer made by Prime Minister Ehud Barak, he could not have done so without peril to his life. In all likelihood, he would have been overthrown or assassinated, as was Anwar Sadat for his heretical effort to make peace with Jews. But the point is moot. Employing several militias under his control, Arafat entered into competition with Hamas and Islamic Jihad in initiating murderous attacks on Israeli citizens wherever they might be found.

The logic is not difficult to grasp. As the Italian journalist

Fiamma Nirenstein explained in a much-discussed essay, Israel in the Arab consciousness

> has been transformed into little more than a diabolical abstraction, not a country at all but a malignant force embodying every possible negative attribute—aggressor, usurper, sinner, occupier, corrupter, infidel, murderer, barbarian. As for Israelis themselves, they are seen not as citizens, workers, students, or parents but as the uniformed foot soldiers of that same dark force.[83]

It is this vision of Israel and Israelis as a diabolical abstraction that explains, in the title of Nirenstein's article, "How Suicide Bombers Are Made." The production of dozens—if not by now hundreds—of such bombers, willing to sacrifice their own lives so long as they can take as many Jews as possible with them, is one salient result of the unceasing vilification.

The targets of such attacks are overwhelmingly Israeli civilians, like the 18-month-old toddler and her 56-year-old grandmother who perished when a suicide bomber detonated himself in an ice cream parlor in a Tel Aviv suburb. But then, Palestinian terrorists and their supporters make a deliberate point of not distinguishing between soldiers and civilians. *Everyone* in Israel, explained Syria's president Bashar Assad in the aftermath of a June 2002 bus bombing in northern Israel, is by definition a member of the Israeli Defense Force and hence a legitimate target.

This justification is not distant in content or spirit from the rationale for killing Jewish civilians put forward by one of the principal architects of the Final Solution, Heinrich Himmler: "I didn't consider I had the right to eradicate the men—that is, to kill them or have them killed—and leave the children to grow up and take revenge on our sons and grandsons."[87] Two decades ago, the Egyptian daily *Al-Ahram* spelled out the same rationale in more colorful detail:

> The first thing that we have to make clear is that no distinction must be made between the Jew and the Israeli.... The Jew is a Jew, through the millennia...in spurning all moral values,

devouring the living and drinking his blood for the sake of a few coins. The Jew, the Merchant of Venice, does not differ from the killer of Deir Yasin or the killer of the camps. There are equal examples of human degradation. Let us therefore put aside such distinctions, and talk about Jews.[85]

The parallels between Nazism and the current Arab-Muslim brand of anti-Semitism are striking. In an incident on the West Bank near the beginning of the intifada, two Israeli soldiers who had lost their way were detained, brought into a Palestinian police station, set upon, stabbed and stomped to death by a frenzied mob. Videotapes of this lynching showed "a body dangling from the second story window of the police station" and "a euphoric man, grinning out the window and holding up his hands stained bright crimson with blood."[86] Outside, Palestinian youths, according to the *New York Times,* chanted in unison, "Here is where we gouged his eyes! Here is where we ripped off his legs! Here is where we smashed in his face!"[87] This is the language not only of Ramallah but also of Auschwitz, where guards engaged in sadistic recreation with their Jewish prisoners.

In the West Bank city of Nablus, a museum celebrates the handiwork of a suicide bomber who killed fifteen Israelis and injured dozens in a pizzeria in Jerusalem. One display offers a reconstruction of the terrorist explosion, "complete with fake body parts and pizza slices strewn all over." Another, showing a large rock in front of a figure wearing the traditional garb of Hasidic Jews, is accompanied by a sound recording: "O believer, there is a Jewish man behind me. Come and kill him."[88] If there is a difference (aside from capability) between the Nazis and the Palestinians, it is that the former kept their murderous intentions a tightly wrapped secret. The soldiers of the SS were hailed as model Aryans by the regime, but their role in creating and running the death camps was not something the Nazis ever chose to advertise. By contrast, the Palestinians trumpet their murderous intentions on the airwaves and in the classroom and gruesomely celebrate their triumphs.

❖

Among Arabs and Muslims, the Palestinians are not alone in translating their anti-Semitism into homicidal action. Regimes across the Middle East have been sponsoring the murder of Jews, in Israel and throughout the world. Prominent among them is Iran. When one considers that Israel and Iran have historically had a common enemy in Iraq, and that Iran and Israel were in an open strategic alliance before the Iranian Revolution of 1979, the intensity and duration of the Iranian enmity toward Israel and toward Jews can be explained only in ideological/theological terms. Hostility toward Israel, reports the *New York Times,* "is one of the litmus tests of loyalty toward the Islamic system in Iran."[89] For more than two decades now, the ayatollahs governing Iran have, like the radical Arab states, attempted to turn their words of hatred into deeds.

One of the most notorious such deeds was the July 18, 1994, destruction of the AMIA Jewish center in faraway Argentina, leaving eighty-five people dead, wounding more than two hundred, and obliterating the archives and library that had served as the institutional memory of the largest Jewish community in South America. Though Iranian authorities continue to deny a role in the attack, a wealth of evidence convincingly suggests that the bombing was organized at the Iranian embassy in Buenos Aires and supervised by a ranking official in the Iranian intelligence service. Terrorism directed against a Jewish community thousands of miles from Iranian shores is perhaps the most powerful testimony of the deep-seated convictions of the Tehran regime.

More evidence exists in the semicovert warfare that the Iranians have been waging against Israel, primarily by way of terrorist proxies in Lebanon but increasingly through forces recruited or infiltrated into the West Bank and Gaza. To organizations like Hizbollah, Hamas, Islamic Jihad and the Popular Front for the Liberation of Palestine–General Command, the Iranians provide financial support, military training and weapons, in return for which they exert considerable leverage and control. Bleeding Israel heavily, Iran succeeded in compelling its withdrawal in 2000 from the buffer zone it had established in southern Lebanon—a submission to force that emboldened the Palestinians to launch the 2000 intifada.

Since then, Iran and Iranian-backed forces have stepped up pressure on the Jewish state. In training camps set up across the Bekaa valley in Lebanon, Iranian specialists have been instructing militants in the arts of mayhem and murder, with particular emphasis on bombs capable of bringing down large structures or igniting fuel depots in so-called megaterrorist attacks. A direct Iranian role in the Palestinian intifada was highlighted in January 2002 in the affair of the *Karine-A,* a ship destined for the Gaza Strip from an Iranian port, laden with an enormous quantity of sophisticated weapons including anti-tank missiles.

One exceptionally well-informed observer of the Iranians is Dennis Ross, who served for eight years as President Clinton's Middle East envoy and who wrote in the summer of 2002 that Iran was "pushing Hamas very hard to continue the suicide bombings in Israel." One reason for this, Ross speculated, may have been a desire to deflect the attention of Washington from its pursuit of the "axis of evil" by intensifying the Palestinian-Israeli conflict. But another, more direct possibility was that the Iranians "believe Israel will lose its resolve and gradually be weakened to the point of collapse," and they "seem prepared to fight to the last Palestinian to produce such an eventuality."[90] Ross expressed puzzlement over another element in Iranian behavior—the buildup of longer-range rockets in southern Lebanon; but this too is fully compatible with the same goal. In January 2002, Israeli foreign minister Shimon Peres estimated that some ten thousand such rockets, all with a range capable of striking cities in northern Israel, were already in place, and by summer the number had grown. Iran's provision of such rockets is completely in accord with a policy toward Jews and Israel that is being pursued for its own sake rather than for any strategic advantage in the region.

The exact same objective is also clearly discernible in

Tehran's determined effort to acquire unconventional weapons of mass destruction and the means of delivering them. Iran is already in possession of a missile, the Shahab 3, capable of striking all of Israel and points beyond, and is believed to be working on longer-range and more accurate systems. On numerous occasions, Iranian officials have threatened Israel with annihilation. The former president, Ayatollah Ali Akbar Hashemi Rafsanjani, who is today the speaker of the national assembly, has publicly noted that "the use of even one nuclear bomb inside Israel will destroy everything." And he adds, "It is not irrational to contemplate such an eventuality."[91]

❖

Far more spectacular than Iran's efforts has been the handiwork of al-Qaeda, whose feats of destruction are known to the entire world. What is far less well known is the obsession of this terrorist organization with the Jews, an obsession reflected in their hatred not only of Israel but also of the United States, and even in their choice of targets.

Anti-Semitism appears to be either a main theme of al-Qaeda training and indoctrination or one of the ideological modes of thought that draw in new members and fellow travelers. It will undoubtedly be decades before transcripts of the interrogations of al-Qaeda detainees at Guantanamo, Cuba, are declassified and released to the public, but insight into the views of associates, recruiters and operatives is to be had from court transcripts, public statements and news reporting. The pieces of the puzzle are fragmented, but the composite picture is unmistakable.

Ramzi Binalshibh was apprehended in Pakistan in 2002 and turned over to U.S. forces. He is suspected of being a possible "twentieth hijacker"; his plan to enter the United States for pilot training was foiled when he was denied a visa. Although little is known about his views, a videotape in possession of the authorities depicts a wedding, apparently in Europe, where Binalshibh was recorded warning loudly of the danger posed by Jews.

Raed Hijazi—an American citizen, a former Boston cab driver, and an al-Qaeda agent—was arrested in Syria in 1999 on charges of "conspiracy to carry out attacks on tourists, notably Jews" during the millennium celebrations. Extradited to Jordan and put on trial in Amman in 2001, Hijazi explained that Ariel Sharon was behind the attacks of September 11: "The proof is that 4,000 Jews who work at the World Trade Center did not go to work that day." His father characterized Hijazi as "a typical American,"[92] and averred that Jordan, in putting him on trial, was only trying to please the "Jews and prove loyalty to them."[93]

Richard Reid attempted to blow up an Air France plane bound from Paris to Florida by igniting explosives concealed in his shoe. After his arrest, he told his interrogators that he formed his plan after a visit to Israel, where he supposedly observed "Jews with guns" inside Jerusalem's al-Aqsa mosque. Asked why he did not attack Israel directly, Reid responded, "Without America there would be no Israel."[94]

A fuller and more revealing case is that of Zacarias Moussaoui, arrested in Minnesota on an immigration violation three weeks before September 11 and suspected of being another missing hijacker. Raised in France and trained by al-Qaeda in Afghanistan, Moussaoui has given vent to a steady stream of anti-Jewish invective in his appearances in court and in documents filed in his case. "I am a Muslim fundamentalist," he has declared, "openly hostile to the Jews and the United States of America." His attorneys' insistence that he undergo an examination for mental competence generated a blast from Moussaoui at this "blasphemous psychiatric so-called evaluation" based upon "obscene Jewish science." The Jews, he offers, have "incurred the curse of Allah and his wrath at those he transformed into monkeys and swine."[95]

As we have seen, such language does not emerge from thin air. Moussaoui, like Richard Reid, is a disciple of sheikhs who served as recruiters for al-Qaeda and its affiliates while preaching the most radical brand of anti-Semitism there is. One such sheikh is Abu Hamza al-Masri, who lost an eye and both hands to injuries he says he incurred while fighting the Soviet occupation of Afghanistan. At London's Finsbury Park mosque, where Abu Hamza presided until the British authorities shut it down, videos show Taliban soldiers slashing, shooting and decapitating captured Northern Alliance soldiers as the voiceover explains that "the war against the Jews and the Christians is being won" and implores viewers to "kill in the name of Allah until you are killed."[96] Al-Masri, still preaching in the aftermath of September 11, insisted that the World Trade Center attack was organized by Jews, that Jewish employees there had advance warning of the attack, and that most of those who perished on that day were Muslims.

Another figure associated with both Moussaoui and Reid is the Jamaican-born Sheikh Abdullah al-Faisal, who lectures in British cities. Among the tapes he has circulated is one listing nineteen reasons why Muslims cannot live in harmony with the "filthy Jews," who are "evil to the core" and "deceitful by nature." Entitled "No Peace with the Jews," the tape includes a question-and-answer session with the following exchange: "Should we hate Jews and when we see them on the street, should we beat them up?" Response: "You have no choice but to hate them. How do you fight the Jews? You kill the Jews."[97] Sheikh al-Faisal, it is worthy of note, studied Islam for eight years in Saudi Arabia.

We may never learn the inner thoughts of Mohammed Atta and the other eighteen hijackers who took their own lives along with those of several thousand others. But we do know that, along with two of his September 11 compatriots, Atta frequented the al-Quds mosque in Hamburg, Germany, where an imam known only by his surname of al-Fazazi preached radical anti-Semitism along with hatred of Christians and the United States, insisting in one videotaped sermon that "Jews and Crusaders should have their throats slit."[98] Al-Fazazi has since fled, but the same brand of preaching continues at the al-Quds mosque. In a tape obtained by the *Washington Post,* the new imam issues a summons "for mortal combat against 'Jews, Israel, and all unbelievers.' "[99]

❖

Moving several rungs up al-Qaeda's ladder of command, we come to Ayman al-Zawahiri, Osama bin Laden's right hand and chief theoretician, and—to close a circle opened earlier—a close student of Sayyid Qutb. Up until 1998, al-Zawahiri was a leading figure in Egyptian Islamic Jihad, an organization that is itself an offspring of Qutb's Muslim Brotherhood and whose principal objective is to fight "the enemies of Islam," among whom al-Zawahiri has listed Americans and Jews in first place. In 1998, al-Zawahiri brought Egyptian Islamic Jihad into a union with al-Qaeda, calling the new organization the International Islamic Front for Jihad against Jews and Crusaders.

To judge by his writings and public pronouncements, al-Zawahiri himself is obsessed with Jewish power and the supposed Jewish threat to Islam. He denounces "the world's Jewish government," which he claims is behind anti-Islamic movements around the world: in Russia, where "Jewish security experts" helped to conduct the war against Chechens; in Egypt, where the government of Hosni Mubarak is a "cornerstone of Jewish expansion in the region"; and in the United States and the West, where "Jews are in control of the media and propaganda tools." No wonder al-Zawahiri calls for "stepping up the jihad action to harm the U.S. and Jewish interests."[100]

The Jews loom just as threatening in the mind of Osama bin Laden. "The enmity between us and the Jews," he said in a 1998 interview, "goes far back in time and is deep rooted. There is no question that war between the two of us is inevitable."[101] Though much of bin Laden's most incendiary rhetoric is aimed specifically at the United States, the distinction between America and the Jews is blurred in his thinking. As he sees it, the two are tightly intertwined, forming what he calls a "Judeo-American alliance."[102]

In his "Letter to the American People," a document evidently written in late 2002, bin Laden focuses on the American tie with Israel:

> The creation and continuation of Israel is one of the greatest crimes, and you [the American people] are the leaders of its criminals. And of course there is no need to explain and prove the degree of American support for Israel. The creation of Israel is a crime which must be erased. Each and every person whose hands have become polluted in the contribution toward this crime must pay its price, and pay for it heavily.[103]

But in bin Laden's conception, the United States is not the prime mover in this relationship; rather, its leaders have "fallen victim to Jewish Zionist blackmail." Therefore, if Americans "cherish their lives and if they cherish their sons," they must change their ways and "elect an American patriotic government that caters to their interests, not the interests of the Jews." Otherwise, they will be faced with unrelenting jihad.[104]

❖

Is there any evidence that hatred of Jews influenced al-Qaeda's choice of targets on September 11? It is clear, of course, that its previous assaults—on American embassies in Tanzania and Kenya, on the USS *Cole* in Yemen—had little direct connection to Jews. But a series of other acts reveal a somewhat different pattern.

One highly suggestive early incident was the 1990 assassination of Rabbi Meir Kahane by an Islamic militant named El Sayyid Nosair. Al-Qaeda had, at this juncture, not yet come into being; it took shape as an organized body somewhat later in the first half of the 1990s. But we can see in Nosair and some of his associates a segment of the structure as it was being built.

The initial New York Police Department investigation of Nosair concluded that he was operating on his own. He was acquitted of the murder of Kahane by a New York jury in 1991. But in 1993, after the truck bombing of the World Trade Center was shown to be the work of a cell of Arab terrorists, the police looked anew at a trove of documents in Arabic that had been seized from Nosair's apartment but not yet translated or studied. They revealed links to this broader conspiracy.

In 1995, Nosair was put on trial once again and convicted

The Return of Anti-Semitism

of seditious conspiracy for plotting a series of bombings of landmarks in New York City, including the George Washington Bridge, the United Nations and the Lincoln and Holland Tunnels. Among his fellow conspirators were the blind sheikh Omar Abdel Rahman and Wadih al-Hage. Both were key figures in al-Qaeda until they too were put on trial, convicted and incarcerated.

The murder of Kahane was by no means the only assault on Jews by the nascent al-Qaeda organization. The first World Trade Center bombing itself, one of the deadliest acts of terrorism on American soil up to that point, was considered by its perpetrators to be an attack on Jews. According to one of them, Abdul Rahman Yasin, today a figure high on the FBI's most-wanted terrorist list, the initial goal of the plot's chief planner, Ramzi Yousef, was "to blow up Jewish neighborhoods in Brooklyn." But then a more inviting target presented itself. "I have an idea," Yousef announced as the plotting was under way. "We should do one big explosion, rather than do small ones in Jewish neighborhoods." The final target was selected because the "majority of the people who work in the World Trade Center are Jews."[105]

On February 26, 1993, a truck carrying a huge quantity of explosives was duly driven into the basement of the World Trade Center and detonated. The bombing killed six people and injured more than a thousand. True, it did not succeed in its primary objective of knocking down one of the Twin Towers, but that ambitious idea had nevertheless been set in motion. Planning for a renewed attempt commenced, it is believed, in late 1998—the same year, we learn from a penetrating inquiry by Lawrence Wright, that "Zawahiri commissioned a study on the Jewish influence in America."[106] The results of that study led the newly constituted International Islamic Front for Jihad against Jews and Crusaders to place the territory of the United States within its sights.

To be sure, al-Qaeda had other grievances against us— including, preeminently, the fact that American troops were stationed on the holy soil of Saudi Arabia. But however disparate these matters might seem to *us,* it is not so clear that al-Qaeda's leading thinkers saw them as other than one and the same. In the opinion of Kay Nehm, the German prosecutor responsible for bringing to justice al-Qaeda operatives apprehended in his country for their part in organizing September 11, all of the perpetrators were united by a seamless "hatred of world Jewry and the United States."[107] Indeed, at the trial of one of these operatives—a man named Mounir el-Motassadeq who was found guilty of 3,066 counts of accessory to murder—one key witness recounted statements he had heard the defendant utter in the run-up to September 11. "They want to do something big" on American soil, the witness recalled hearing. "The Jews will burn and we will dance on their graves."[108]

As planning for the September 11 attack was beginning, al-Zawahiri himself explained al-Qaeda's rationale for existence in the jihadist journal *Al-Mujahidoun:*

> America is now controlled by the Jews, completely, as are its news, its elections, its economy, and its politics. It uses Israel to attack its neighbors and to slaughter those who are living peacefully there.... If we are a nation of martyrs—as we claim—all that we need is courage of heart and the will of killers and the belief in what we claim to be love of death for Allah's sake. That is the key to our triumph and the beginning of their defeat. If you want to live as free people and to die in honor and be sent as martyrs, the road in front of you is clear.[109]

❖

If the bloody history of the last century teaches a single lesson, it is that we must take seriously the words of political leaders who openly proclaim murder as their goal. Alan Bullock, the great historian and biographer of Hitler, pointed to one of the most extraordinary features of the German tyrant: "Hitler's originality lay not in his ideas, but in the terrifyingly literal way in which he set to work to translate fantasy into reality, and in his unequaled grasp of the means by which to do this."[110]

Hitler's fantasy was elaborated in *Mein Kampf,* written in 1923–24 and published in millions of copies in the 1930s for all the world to see. So too are the fantasies of the Islamic militants on display to the entire world, and so have they been for a long time. Al-Zawahiri writes:

> Tracking down the Americans and the Jews is not impossible. Killing them with a single bullet, a stab, or a device made up of a popular mix of explosives or hitting them with an iron rod is not impossible.... With the available means, small groups could prove to be a frightening horror for the Americans and the Jews.[111]

Out of this infernal stew, in which anti-Semitism was a prime ingredient, the plot of September 11 was conceived, came into being, and was executed.

❖

THREE

EUROPE REVERTS

Like everything else in nature, anti-Semitism abhors a vacuum. The Muslim and Arab world may be the engine of
today's resurgence of this ancient and incendiary hatred, as well
as the locus of some of its most violent forms of expression. But
even there, let alone elsewhere, anti-Semitism could not flour-
ish so luxuriantly were it not for two other factors. The first is
the role played by governments within the Muslim-Arab orbit,
some of which actively foment anti-Semitism, others of which
support and encourage it, and all of which fail to condemn or
suppress it. The second is the role played by the "civilized"
West, especially Europe.

The wheel of history has indeed rotated. Over a period
of centuries, Europe was a net exporter of homegrown anti-
Semitism, with its product line enjoying especially strong
demand in the Islamic world. As we have seen in Part Two, the
latter entity has now taken over the position of global manu-
facturer and supplier—with a vengeance. But to complete the
circle, Europe has today become an eager importer, its old
deadly goods being shipped back to it in a variety of forms and
along a number of channels, and finding a disturbingly ready
market.

With its relatively open borders and its cosmopolitan cultural life, modern Europe is highly permeable. Through the
steady flow of immigrants and the infiltration of determined

militants, it has managed to absorb a contingent of fanatical anti-Semitic murderers, as the unraveling roots of the September 11 plot have made evident. But that is hardly the extent of the continent's new Jewish problem. For the influx of foreign influences has reawakened older, more established and more native attitudes. The fires of the Crusades, the trials and tortures of the Inquisition, the expulsions of Jews from country after country, the culmination of the anti-Semitic tradition in Hitler's crematoria—all of these terrible events, far from acting as a check, seem to have prepared fertile ground for dormant seeds of evil to germinate once again.

Physical violence is the most obvious manifestation of the new European reality. Over the 1980s and especially the 1990s, from Hamburg to Bosnia, from Milan to London, small cells of Muslim fundamentalists, operating under the umbrella structure of al-Qaeda, entered Europe to engage in terrorism and armed subversion. Much of the activity of this loose pan-European coalition has been devoted to waging a global war against the Jews. The first major terrorist assault planned and executed from Europe after September 11 occurred when a Muslim fundamentalist named Nizar bin Muhammed Nawar, coordinating his movements with a German-born Pole, drove a propane-laden truck into a 2,000-year-old synagogue on the Tunisian island of Djerba, killing seventeen tourists in a fiery blast. It did not take long for German intelligence to ascertain that the bombing was the handiwork of an organization known as the Tunisian Fighting Group, an al-Qaeda affiliate that has been operating out of Hamburg and northern France. Eight suspects later arrested in Lyons, France, were also connected to the bombing.

The attack on the Djerba synagogue was the deadliest of a string of planned assaults. Other plots, either against Jewish targets or motivated by hatred of Jews, were disrupted by European police forces before they could be carried out. A number of them have been the work of groups with no formal ties to al-Qaeda but operating in support of the movement's objectives. On September 7, 2002, for example, German police arrested a Turkish couple who were planning to attack a U.S. military base near Heidelberg with the aid of pipe bombs they had assembled in their apartment. Both were self-professed admirers of Osama bin Laden; the man was described as harboring "a hatred for Americans and Jews."[1]

In the same month, twelve members of a pan-European "Arab-Mujahedeen network" were arrested by Germany's equivalent of the FBI as they were drafting operations to coincide with the first anniversary of September 11, involving "strikes against Israeli or Jewish institutions in Germany."[2] Eight of the twelve suspects appeared to be members of a Palestinian fundamentalist group based in Britain.

Then there was the plan, also foiled by German police, "to blow up a Jewish synagogue in France"—the description of the objective supplied by one of the perpetrators, an Algerian named Aeurobui Beandali who received military training and political indoctrination in an al-Qaeda camp in Afghanistan. In April 2002, he and four others were arrested in Germany. Police found in their possession a storehouse of guns, grenades, detonation caps and bomb-making chemicals, and were able to disclose links between this group and underground cells in Britain, France and Italy. At trial, Beandali testified that his group "planned to destroy the synagogue after Sabbath prayers."[3] One of his codefendants denounced the court with the most cutting words in his lexicon: "Look at the judge's face," he shouted as he was being hauled out of the courtroom. "These people are just Jews."[4]

❖

It is highly unlikely that these incidents exhaust the list of recent terrorist attacks on Jewish targets or attacks motivated in part or in full by hatred of Jews. In Germany alone, the police estimate that some 59,100 foreigners belong to 65 groups with extremist proclivities. They have already been compelled to launch some 72 separate investigations in the wake of September 11; other inquiries are continuing in every European nation. Much more information will undoubtedly emerge, but what is already clear is that even if the radical Islamic fundamentalists who have infiltrated European society turn out to be relatively few in number—in the hundreds, not the thousands—they are elements of a much broader community that gives them shelter and succor and works to encourage other forms of physical violence against Jews.

The community to which I am referring is the rapidly expanding one of Islamic immigrants to Europe, which has changed the face of the continent irreversibly. The numbers alone are an important part of the story. Five decades ago, there were fewer than a million Muslims in Europe. Today there are no fewer than fifteen million, and perhaps as many as twenty million. The continent is becoming partly Islamicized.

France is the most striking case. In 1995, according to a study in *Le Monde,* there were three to four million Muslims in the country.[5] Thanks to a high birthrate and continuing immigration, a more accurate figure today would be about six million, which is 10 percent of France's population. French Muslims now outnumber French Jews by ten to one, and their growing presence has had a marked impact on the religious, political and cultural balance of the country.

The changes taking place in France are typical and, with variations, visible across the continent; everywhere, they include a strong element of anti-Semitism. To begin with, the Muslim population on average is faring poorly according to almost every indicator of integration and success. In France, approximately half of unemployed workers are Muslim, a rate more than double the national average. Those who do succeed in gaining employment are mostly concentrated in low-paying, low-prestige, unskilled jobs.

Housing for Muslims is universally bleak and over-crowded. A large fraction of France's Muslims live in urban *foyers,* dismal housing projects for unaccompanied foreign workers that are seedbeds of violence and criminality. French leftist intellectuals often lecture the United States about the disproportionate number of blacks in American prisons, but incarceration rates in France are no less strikingly "out of balance": over half of prison inmates and 43 percent of the residents of juvenile justice facilities are "foreign-born," a euphemism for Muslim.[6]

Reflecting the country's colonial past, French Muslims are overwhelmingly North African, primarily from Algeria and Morocco. In neighboring Germany, where two million Turks comprise the single largest group among the roughly three million Muslims, the picture is little different. Along with a sizable number of Moroccans and Tunisians, Germany's Turks were brought in as "guest workers" in the 1960s, a temporary arrangement that has long since become permanent; generations of Turks and Arabs have been born on German soil and, as elsewhere, they are not faring well. According to a recent survey, "a high percentage" of Germany's Muslim immigrants are "threatened by job losses," and unemployment among this group "has risen disproportionately." School dropout rates are far higher than the German norm; even for those with a higher education, "the prospects of finding jobs" are bleaker than for Germans. Most of Germany's Muslims live in what are described as "cheap accommodation and rented flats in run-down neighborhoods, where few Germans would reside," resulting in the emergence of "Turkish/Muslim ghettos."[7]

In England—where Pakistanis and Bangladeshis make up the largest component of the Muslim community—one study reports severe disadvantages in the labor market. Four out of five Muslim households "have an income equivalent to less than half the national average." Educational opportunities are abysmal, educational attainments correspondingly poor. Housing conditions mirror those across the Channel. The crime-ridden neighborhoods of Asian Muslims are characterized as "the worst types of urban housing complexes."[8]

One could usefully survey Italy, Holland, Spain and a dozen or so other European countries. But the overall trend is clear. In purely material terms, Europe's large and growing Muslim population lags woefully behind, a fact that is itself a significant coefficient of alienation and resentment. Yet material hardships are only a part of the story, and by no means the most crucial. Europe's Islamic population, even as it grows in numbers, has nowhere been assimilated into the cultural and social fabric of European life. And if the immigrants are disaffected and resentful—or positively hostile to European ways—the surrounding European population feels a mutual aversion. This is plainly visible in politics, as can be seen in the rise of Jorg Haider's Freedom Party in Austria or Jean-Marie Le Pen's National Front in France. In 2002, running largely on an anti-immigrant platform and at a moment when, according to pollsters, a full two-thirds of Frenchmen believed there were "too many Arabs" in the country, Le Pen succeeded in garnering enough votes to force Prime Minister Jacques Chirac into a runoff, an unprecedented achievement.

But the antipathy is reciprocal. An alternative non- or anti-European identity has come to the fore among Europe's Muslims, and that identity is Islam itself. At soccer matches, it is not the European players who draw cheers from young European Muslims but visiting Arab teams; the French national team has been jeered and pelted with bottles by French North Africans. Among many Muslim females, wearing a chador has become a means of asserting self- and peoplehood, and has emerged as a potent symbol of defiance.[9] Although more than 85 percent of the French population favors banning the use of Islamic headgear in public schools, such restrictions, where they have been put in place, have led only to further radicalization.

❖

This is not the whole story, of course. Undoubtedly, the majority of Europe's Muslims are traditionalists who practice what might be called a quietist form of Islam, almost entirely apolitical. A number of Muslim leaders have spoken out against more radical currents, and have sought to find a way to integrate Islam into the fabric of European life. But the traditionalist segment is not the dynamic segment; a rapidly growing cadre in Europe, as in the Middle East, stresses the need to embrace more stringent observance of the faith and is also striving to expand the sweep of territory subject to "genuine" Islamic rule. Numerical estimates are hard to come by, but there is no question that the fundamentalist tendency is increasingly dominant among the young in a population that, thanks to a high birthrate, is becoming more youthful by the day.

This is the brand of Islam that also serves as the major conduit into Europe of the Middle Eastern brand of anti-Semitism. It acts both by cultural osmosis and by deliberate impetus from governments. Saudi Arabia, for one, has been working assiduously to establish the Wahhabi brand of Islam in European countries. The government-run Saudi news magazine *Ain al-Yaqeen* credits the royal family with having established some 1,500 mosques, an unspecified number of Islamic "cultural" and "academic" centers, and 202 colleges and 2,000 schools "for educating Muslim children" the world over. European cities that enjoy the largesse of the royal family include Brussels, Madrid, London, Lyons, Edinburgh, Zagreb, Moscow, Lisbon and Vienna. Rome's Islamic center features a mosque, a library and a lecture hall, all paid for personally by King Fahd, whose $50 million donation toward the cost of construction has been supplemented with an annual contribution of $1.5 million for upkeep. No less generously supported is the facility in Malaga, Spain, the seat of the King Fahd Islamic Center—a "university-like" facility that "embraces academic, educational, cultural, and propagatory [i.e., propaganda] activities."[10]

Saudi Arabia is the largest Arab benefactor, but it is not alone in these "propagatory" activities. Other participants in this "invasion by proxy," as it has been called, include Kuwait, the United Arab Emirates, Syria and Iran, all of which have funded centers and mosques of their own and underwritten individual imams, scholars, conferences and the like. In Hamburg, for example, one finds the Shiite Ali mosque, an institution established during the reign of the shah of Iran, which after the Iranian Revolution became a German outpost for the propaganda and espionage operations of the mullahs.[11]

States are not the only sponsors of the proxy invasion;

subnational groups have been avidly setting up their own parallel structures. In England, radical movements like the Egyptian Islamic Group, an organization on the U.S. State Department list of terrorist organizations, remain free to carry out their work relatively untrammeled. Hizbollah and Hamas both maintain political and financial operations in the United Kingdom, and a figure like the Palestinian terrorist Leila Khaled, arrested but never tried for her role in the 1970 hijacking of an El Al airliner, has been invited to give public lectures. (Khaled informed an audience at the London School of Economics that "there are no suicide bombers; they are all freedom fighters.")[12] Also at large in England is the radical organization al-Muhajiroun, led by the Syrian-born Sheikh Omar Bakri Mohammed, who at a rally on the first anniversary of September 11 declared of bin Laden: "I believe this man stands for a just cause."[13]

The Muslim Brotherhood of Sayyid Qutb is also a significant part of the story. As long ago as 1954, following the fall of King Farouk in Egypt and upheavals in Syria and across the region, West Germany became a point of refuge for Islamists fleeing persecution in the Middle East. Among those who took up residence in the city of Aachen were Sayyid Ramadan, the ranking leader of the Egyptian Muslim Brotherhood, and Essam al-Attar, his Syrian counterpart. Three decades later, perhaps as many as ten thousand members of the movement had come to settle in Aachen, turning it into what the scholar Khalid Duran has called "Europe's No. 1 stronghold of jihadism."[14] As we know from post-9/11 investigations, other centers in Munich and Hamburg have been no less zealous in their propaganda activities, not to mention in the actual plotting of terrorist actions.

❖

Notable is the way in which European converts to Islam have been drawn into these radical groups. I have already mentioned the shoe-bomber Richard Reid, of mixed Jamaican-British origin, who tried to bring down a Boeing 747 midway over the

64

Atlantic Ocean. Another instructive example is Christian Ganczarski, the German-Pole who was connected to the bombing of the synagogue in Djerba.

According to a police deposition obtained by the *Wall Street Journal*, Ganczarski, who converted to Islam in 1986, was working as an apprentice welder in 1991 in Germany's Ruhr Valley when he fell under the influence of Nadeem Elyas, the head of Germany's Central Council of Muslims. After preliminary meetings in Aachen, he was persuaded to travel to Medina, Saudi Arabia, and enroll there in a course of Islamic studies. The idea, Ganczarski later told German interrogators, was that "non-Arab converts would be educated at this university and learn Islam so that they later could teach Islam to non-Arabs in their homelands and serve as a role model."[15]

In the event, the attempt to indoctrinate Ganczarski in the Wahhabi brand of Islam proved only partly successful: he was too poor a student to complete his education. But he was nonetheless radicalized by the experience, and after returning to Germany, he undertook visits to Chechnya, Pakistan and Afghanistan, where he made contacts with al-Qaeda operatives. In the months following September 11, Ganczarski was tracked by the German authorities and finally arrested on April 15, 2002. A police search of his apartment yielded an address book containing the telephone number of Ramzi Muhammad Abdullah Binalshibh, a fugitive Yemeni terrorist thought to be one of the key planners of the September 11 attack. Subsequently released for lack of sufficient inculpatory evidence, he was allowed to leave Germany for Saudi Arabia. In June 2003, a year after the Tunisian bombing, Saudi Arabia expelled Ganczarski to Germany under American pressure and he was arrested by French police en route.

Still another and even more significant case—not because it is connected to violence but because it illustrates the way that ideas cross borders—is that of Shaykh Abdalqadir as-Sufi of Scotland, a former bit-part actor previously known as Ian Neil Dallas. Having converted to Islam over three decades ago, Dallas emerged in the 1990s as the leader of the Murabitun, a sect headquartered in an enormous mansion in Inverness. This group reportedly numbers in the hundreds. Almost all of its members are European converts to the faith—men like Ahmad Thompson, a British-born barrister who practices law in Norwich, and Yassin Dutton (a.k.a. Stuart Michael Dutton), a lecturer in Islamic studies at Edinburgh University. Despite its modest numbers, the Murabitun has managed to open branches across the world, including elsewhere in the United Kingdom, in Spain, Germany, Switzerland, South Africa and the United States—all ostensibly devoted to finding an Islamic solution to the "many and urgent economic, ecological, and social problems facing the world." But the Murabitun has another agenda as well: fanatical anti-Semitism.

In publications and videos, the Murabitun has made its message plain. One part has to do with pointing out how Jews control the world, operating through what Shaykh Abdalqadir characterizes as "an unelected banking elite" and by means of a "masonic ethos" that "has enslaved the Muslims, treated them like dogs, and degraded them." What is necessary, therefore, is a jihad against "the world-networked usury system of banks and stock-exchange control." Among the outstanding jihadists of modern times, according to one 1991 video issued by the group, is none other than Adolf Hitler, a man of "great genius and great vision."

In publications issued by this movement, one will learn that "no scientific mind accepts the fantastical figure of six million gassed" in Nazi camps. Readers are implored to "grasp what jewism [*sic*] is doing while hiding under the smokescreen of self-orchestrated holocaust propaganda." And what is "jewism" doing, if not cloaking Jewish criminality perpetrated especially by the state of Israel? Arab prisoners in Israel "are treated to much worse degradation than was even known to the Waffen SS all those long years ago," while Palestinian refugees have been "genocidally destroyed by the agents of those same Jews who perpetually whine about the alleged massacre of their people for the crime of usury in Europe in the 30's."[16]

In composition, the Murabitun is almost wholly an

indigenous British creation, with a sprinkling of continental Europeans thrown in. But the propaganda it peddles is the same material that is endemic in the Islamic world. In this case as in others, we are dealing not with ideas that have migrated spontaneously across borders, but with sources and resources abroad. As documented by the *Observer* of London, the Murabitun's first mosque, in the city of Norwich, was underwritten by an unnamed "benefactor" from the Persian Gulf. Far larger sums have evidently come from Malaysia, where "backers" donated some £325,000 to enable the group to purchase its headquarters in Inverness.[17] For his part, Shaykh Abdalqadir has been a frequent visitor to Malaysia, where he consorts with that country's principal anti-Semitic voice, Prime Minister Mahathir Mohamad.

❖

The story in Europe is everywhere the same: the music is piped in from abroad, the dancing takes place at home. It assumes the form of highly organized acts of terrorism carried out by Muslim fanatics working in secret cells, and (as we shall see) it assumes different forms as well.

The outbreak of the second Palestinian uprising in September 2000, the so-called al-Aqsa intifada, triggered a swelling tide of spontaneous and/or semi-organized attacks on Jewish symbols, Jewish institutions, and Jews themselves. In the first weeks alone, more than 250 anti-Semitic incidents occurred in Europe. Though the proximate cause of the violence was the Middle East conflict, it was not directed, as one might suppose, at Israeli visitors, Israeli companies or Israeli diplomatic facilities. Rather, it was aimed at European Jews. It occurred in almost every country on the continent, but it was especially evident in peaceful, democratic, law-abiding Western Europe—a part of the world that for quite some time now has prided itself on the personal safety it affords its inhabitants.

It would require a separate book just to rehearse the entire litany, but even a sampling suffices to convey the scope and intensity of the violence. In England and France, the two countries with the most sizable Jewish populations, six synagogues were burned to the ground in the first weeks of the intifada; another twenty-four were the victims of arson attacks. A number of the attacks were timed to coincide with the High Holy Day of Yom Kippur: in Paris, a sniper fired an M-16 rifle into the city's Great Synagogue while services were going on. Elsewhere, Jews walking to synagogue were struck with stones, and even schoolchildren were harassed by assailants. "Three More Synagogues Attacked in France," was the Associated Press headline in mid-October.[18] In Great Britain, a yeshiva student was stabbed on a bus, synagogues in major cities were vandalized, Torah scrolls destroyed.

Elsewhere it was the same. In Antwerp, Belgium, worshippers were cursed and threatened with violence as they walked to synagogue. In Brussels, an elderly Jewish man was set upon and beaten so badly he required hospitalization. Molotov cocktails were hurled into a Düsseldorf synagogue. In the German city of Weimar, vandals dubbed swastikas and smashed windows at a monument commemorating the Buchenwald concentration camp. More windows were smashed at a synagogue in Berlin. Some 250 people in Essen attacked the local synagogue with stones. In the publication *Anti-Semitism Worldwide,* which records all such incidents, one can read of similar violence in every corner of Europe: Salonika, Florence, Venice, Rome, Madrid, Geneva, Emmen and Oss in the Netherlands, Malmö in Sweden.

As severe as it was, this wave turned out to be merely a prelude. A year later, the September 11 terrorist attack *on America* led to a sharp increase in European violence against Jews. According to the authoritative *Anti-Semitism Worldwide,* anti-Semitic incidents in Great Britain "rose by 150 percent in September and October [2001] over August 2001. The figures for September and October were the second and the third highest monthly totals ever recorded. In France, 44 percent of major violent incidents and attacks for the year 2001 took place in September and October."[19]

And the curve rose still higher when, in late March and

April 2002, Israel responded to the ongoing intifada by entering the West Bank in force. That military operation was
precipitated by a months-long campaign of Arab terror within
Israel whose culminating outrage—the bombing of a hotel ball-
room in the central Israeli city of Netanya—had snuffed out
the lives of 29 and injured more than 140 as they sat at their
seder tables on the first night of Passover. The Israeli incursion,
aimed at uncovering and destroying bomb factories and appre-
hending those responsible for the mass killings of civilians, did
not achieve all of its objectives, but it did result in a radical
diminution of terrorist attacks inside the country. It also led to
the seizure of a trove of intelligence information, including
documents confirming that Yasir Arafat, Israel's ostensible
partner in the Oslo peace process—and a man richly subsidized by the European Union—was in possession of arms
forbidden to him by the Oslo Accords and was personally
funding and directing the civilian bombing missions of at least
one armed unit, the al-Aqsa Martyrs Brigade.

❖

Another consequence—perhaps predictable by now—of
Israel's action to defend itself was an upsurge in anti-Semitic
violence *in Europe* unprecedented since the 1930s. From east
to west, the list of incidents in April 2002 alone is too long to
summarize. In the Ukrainian capital of Kiev, some fifty youths
chanting "Kill the kikes" descended on the city's central synagogue on a Saturday evening, broke twenty windows and beat
the director of the religious school with stones.[20] In Greece,
Jewish cemeteries were vandalized in what the press termed
"anti-Jewish acts of revenge," and the Holocaust memorial in
Salonika, a city whose fifty thousand Jews had been rounded
up and deported to Nazi death camps in 1943, was defaced
with Palestinian slogans.[21] In Slovakia, Jewish cemeteries were
desecrated in what an official described as the "biggest attack
on the Jewish community since the Holocaust."[22]

In the heart of democratic Europe, one particular scene
of violent anti-Israel demonstrations was Amsterdam, Holland,

where "protesters" hurled rocks and bottles and small roving bands used stones and bicycles to shatter store windows. In neighboring Belgium, five firebombs were tossed into a synagogue in a working-class district of Brussels, and a Jewish bookstore was severely damaged by arsonists; a synagogue in Antwerp was firebombed with Molotov cocktails, while in the same city, a travel agency specializing in trips to Israel was set alight. In Germany, two Orthodox Jews were beaten while walking on Berlin's chic Kurfürstendamm, in the heart of the shopping district. A woman wearing a Star of David necklace was attacked in the subway. Jewish memorials in Berlin were defaced with swastikas. A synagogue was spray-painted with the words, "Six Million Is Not Enough."[23] Anti-Israel demonstrators hurled bricks through windows as they marched.

In England, reported London's *Express,* "race-hate attacks on the Jewish community have soared."[24] In the first ten days of April there were fifteen anti-Semitic incidents, including eight physical assaults. Most of the attacks were on Jews walking alone, set upon and beaten by small roving bands. At least two of the victims required hospitalization.

But it was France, once again, that lay at the epicenter of aggression. Of that country's four major outbreaks of anti-Semitism over the entire post–World War II era, the latest wave, according to one expert analyst, has been "stronger than all the rest."[25] The *New York Times* concurs with this estimate, characterizing the current situation as "the worst spate of anti-Jewish violence" in France in the last half-century.[26]

The first two weeks of April 2002 alone saw "nearly 360 crimes against Jews and Jewish institutions," according to the French interior ministry.[27] Gangs of hooded men descended on Jewish victims and struck them with iron clubs. Buses carrying Jewish schoolchildren were stoned. Cemeteries were desecrated. Synagogues, Jewish schools, student facilities and kosher stores were defaced, battered and firebombed. On April 1, the Or Aviv synagogue in Marseille was burned to the ground, its prayerbooks and Torah scrolls consumed by flames; it was one of five synagogues in France attacked in that period.

A kosher butcher store was sprayed with gunfire in Toulouse. Near Lyons, an Orthodox couple was assaulted and beaten on the street. At a soccer field in Bondy, a suburb of Paris, a band of thugs wearing masks and wielding iron bars, heavy steel balls and strips of barbed wired descended upon a teenage Jewish soccer team and set to work beating its members while chanting "death to the Jews."[28] The goalkeeper, a fifteen-year-old boy, ended up in a hospital, requiring a half-dozen stitches on his head. In the heart of Paris's Jewish district, a young Jewish boy was held in captivity for two hours, beaten and humiliated before being released.

❖

This inadequate survey of one brief interval is infinitely expandable, for the passage of time has brought new outrages. In general, the pace of violence rises and falls in conjunction with the intensity of the conflict in the Middle East—a linkage that suggests, correctly, that European Muslims dominate the field in the violence. There have been exceptions: in Germany, France and England, some incidents have been the work of neo-Nazi extremists joined by bands of skinheads, and in the former Soviet bloc, particularly in Ukraine and Russia, soccer hoodlums, neonationalists and neofascists are responsible for a major share of attacks. But elsewhere, and particularly in Western Europe, the identity of the perpetrators has been fairly consistent.

The violence in Belgium, as we learn from arrests made there, has been overwhelmingly the work of Arabs. The stoning of the synagogue in Essen occurred during a demonstration organized by the German-Lebanese Friendship Association. The yeshiva student attacked on a bus in London was stabbed by an Algerian, and it was Arabs who desecrated the synagogues in Great Britain. Almost all of the attacks in France, police records suggest, have been at Muslim hands; according to the French minister of the interior, the perpetrators have generally been "Arab youths from North African countries."[29]

Jean Kahn, chairman of the Central Council of Jewish

71

Communities in France, has described the ongoing wave of violence as "a build-up to a new Kristallnacht," referring to the
pogrom unleashed by the Nazis against German Jews on
November 9 and 10, 1938—itself a portent of far worse to
come.[30] As if taking the hint, Jews are indeed fleeing France:
more than 2,500 left in 2002, double the figure of the previous
year, and fully one-quarter of French Jews, according to a
recent poll, have contemplated departure.[31]

One must be cautious in drawing parallels. Unlike in the
1930s, there is no organized power, let alone any European
government, behind today's assaults. In Nazi Germany, the
force of law was mobilized in the service of lawlessness. In
every European country today, the police have generally done
their duty to investigate and halt the crimes. Official hesitation
and vacillation, yes; but these are generally traceable less to
overt or covert anti-Semitism than to timidity in the face of a
growing Muslim population (and a shrinking Jewish one).

Still, even if we are far from 1938, physical violence
against Jews has become a pan-European phenomenon. What
is more, everywhere one turns, this physical violence has been
accompanied, and abetted, by an explosion of verbal violence
that continues unabated and, a mere half-century after the
Holocaust, is itself a stunning occurrence.

The themes are uniform: Israel, a democratic country vic-
timized *by* terrorism, is singled out from all the nations of the
world, many of them viciously oppressive tyrannies, and
accused *of* terrorism. The Jews, having *suffered* the most determined and thoroughgoing genocide in history, stand accused of
perpetrating genocide. The language in which such accusations
are leveled is extravagantly hateful, drawn from the vocabulary of World War II and the Holocaust but grotesquely
inverted, with the Jews portrayed as Nazis and their Arab tormentors cast in the role of helpless Jews. Anti-Semitism is the
right and only word for an anti-Zionism so one-sided, so eager
to indict Israel while exculpating those bent on Israel's destruction, so adroit in the use of moral double standards, so quick to

issue false and baseless charges, and so disposed to paint Israelis and Jews as evil incarnate.

In the spring of 2002, in the course of a mere two weeks, Europe went into a paroxysm of anti-Jewish fervor. Street demonstrations took place not only in every major capital but in hundreds of smaller cities and towns. In Tuzla, a town in Bosnia, some 1,500 demonstrators carried placards reading "Sharon and Hitler, Two Eyes in the Same Head" and "Israel—the Real Face of Terrorism."[32] In Dublin, Ireland, the banners, several featuring Nazi swastikas superimposed over Stars of David, read "Stop the Palestinian Holocaust" and "Jerusalem: Forever Beloved, Forever Palestinian."[33] In Barcelona, Spain, demonstrators carried placards inscribed "Israel Murderer; USA Accomplice" and "No to Genocide." In Paris, the posters read "Hitler Has a Son: Sharon"; in Belgium, "Hitler Had Two Sons: Bush and Sharon."[34] In Salonika, a solidarity concert was staged under the slogan "Stop the Genocide Now—We Are All Palestinians."[35] In Bilbao, Spain, thousands marched through the streets chanting "No to Zionist Terrorism." In Berlin, the placards read "Stop the Genocide in Palestine" and "Sharon Is a Child Murderer."[36] Across Italy one could find ubiquitous graffiti featuring the swastika emblazoned over the Star of David; in Rome, demonstrators dressed as suicide bombers bore posters equating Ariel Sharon with Adolf Hitler. In cities and towns all over France, "Death to Jews" and "Jews—Murderers" were refrains heard at rally after rally.

❖

If Muslims have taken the lead in perpetrating physical violence, others, mostly on the political Left, have led the way in verbal incitement and abuse. At the event in Dublin, organized by a group known as the Ireland-Palestine Solidarity Campaign, half the demonstrators were reportedly Irishmen. In Brussels, not only Arab students but representatives of Belgian social and political organizations took part, including the Catholic movement Pax Christi, the Belgian Socialist Party and the Belgian Green Party. The solidarity concert in Salonika was organized by, among others, two Greek trade-union bodies, while the dean of Athens University lent his strong vocal support. In Barcelona, where some ten thousand people turned out, unions, political parties and nongovernmental organizations campaigned against Israeli "genocide" and set fire to a Star of David. In Italy, "pacifists" were the mainstay of the pro-Palestinian demonstrations. A Jewish member of Italy's pro-Israel Radical Party was beaten—so much for pacifism— at a gay-rights demonstration for attempting to hold aloft an Israeli flag.

In France, at the rallies where chants of "death to the Jews" were heard, one could find, according to Agence France-Presse, not only the Muslim Students of France and the Committee of Moroccan Workers but also officials of various trade unions and members of the Revolutionary Communist League, the Greens and the French Communist Party, along with officials of the Human Rights League. In the front ranks was José Bové, the French environmentalist known best for his campaign against genetically engineered crops and for vandalizing McDonald's hamburger outlets. On French television, Bové suggested that the anti-Semitic violence in his country was the work of Israelis themselves. "Who profits from the crime?" he asked, and then answered: "The Israeli government and its secret services have an interest in creating a certain psychosis, in making believe that there is a climate of anti-Semitism in France, in order to distract attention from what they are doing."[37]

But the street-level scene is only the beginning; it is in the world of elite opinion and high politics that the nature of the European anti-Semitic movement becomes fully evident. Some agitation comes from the Right, especially its far edge, where Nazism and fascism live on in attenuated form in almost all the major Western European countries. There are also religious-nationalist movements that follow an anti-Semitic platform with roots deeply embedded in the past.

In Central and Eastern Europe, this last species of anti-

Semitism is in ample supply. From the Black Hundreds to the Beilis Affair to the Doctors' Plot, Russia has one of the richest histories of anti-Semitic persecution in the world, spanning the czarist and the Soviet eras alike. In the post-Communist epoch, these anti-Semitic traditions have periodically gone underground but hardly seem to have perished. Just as "Jewish" Bolsheviks were blamed by some for the catastrophe of the Communist era, so too are "Jewish" capitalists now blamed by others for the USSR's decline and fall. In quarters of the contemporary Russian press, a common theme is that Jewish financiers—"oligarchs," as they are called—have enriched themselves by ravaging Mother Russia. More than a few literary figures echo such thoughts: in one recent novel, the antihero, a Jewish entrepreneur, is presented sipping champagne while contemplating a plan "to take the blood and organs of the healthy [Russians] and sell them to medical centers in Israel."[38]

Throughout the former Communist world, this sort of thing enjoys varying degrees of success. Right-wing propagandists and parties are highly active, for example, in Hungary, the home of some eighty thousand Jews; in Budapest, bands of skinheads roam at will, often chanting anti-Semitic slogans. The *Magyar Forum,* a particularly venomous weekly, occupies itself with invective against "Satan's Agents," the Jews.[39] A champion of the same orientation is Istvan Csurka, the leader of the Hungarian Justice and Life Party, who declares that Budapest has fallen into "the hands of pushy, selfish Jewish businessmen who, if their interests require, will shepherd their own race to the slaughterhouse."[40] In Poland, where three and a half million Jews once lived and not more than ten thousand remain today, there is a proliferation of small anti-Semitic organizations like National Rebirth of Poland and a range of newspapers, magazines and broadcast outlets offering more of the same.

Again, one must be careful not to exaggerate. If Jewish responsibility for the wounds inflicted by Communism is one major theme, the former Soviet bloc countries have also peered beneath the scars left by their own cruel histories and refused to turn away in denial. In Poland, the publication in 2001 of

Jan T. Gross's *Neighbors,* a historical account of a wartime massacre of Jews by Poles in the town of Jedwabne, opened up an impassioned debate about wartime anti-Semitism and its legacy. Although the debate featured more than a few diehard Polish apologists, it also brought forward honest historians who attempted to assimilate the long-buried facts and place them in a context of historical truth. At the highest level of the government, president Aleksander Kwasniewski, a man who had once served as a functionary of Poland's anti-Semitic Communist regime, issued an unqualified apology for the massacre: "I beg pardon in my own name and the name of those Poles whose conscience is shattered by that crime."[41]

A similar story might be told about Russia: at the grassroots level, anti-Semitism remains entrenched and lethal, but among the ruling elite the story is more complicated. In the summer of 2002, in cities across the former Soviet Union, individuals or perhaps an organized group began to place signs with anti-Jewish slogans along highways and other major thoroughfares. Some of these signs were attached to explosive devices, designed to maim or murder anyone attempting to take them down. The first such booby-trapped placard severely burned twenty-seven-year-old Tatyana Sapunova, a non-Jewish Russian who stopped to pull down a placard bearing the words "Death to the Kikes." Invited by Prime Minister Vladimir Putin to a televised ceremony at the Kremlin, Tatyana Sapunova was honored for her bravery, lauded by the prime minister for setting an "extremely important [example] for the country from a moral point of view," and awarded one of Russia's highest decorations, the Order of Courage.[42] One cannot imagine any such thing under the Communists; up until a mere decade and a half ago, the anti-Semitic signboards would have been hushed up by the authorities—assuming they were not the work of the authorities.

❖

In Western Europe, the Right operates somewhat differently. A school of highbrow revisionist historians has emerged in Germany to offer a sometimes subtle apologia for Hitler and the Third Reich. The leading figures of this school are Ernst Nolte and Andreas Hillgruber, in whose version of the past Germany's war against the Jews was a regrettable if not entirely incomprehensible error. The Jews, after all, had declared their loyalty to the Allied side in 1939, so it was only natural that Hitler should respond to the danger they represented, if by means that were unwarranted and unjustified. What's more, although the crimes he committed constitute a perpetual burden of national shame, they must be placed on a continuum with the atrocities and outrages of the twentieth century's other totalitarian regimes, from Stalin to Mao to Pol Pot; what Hitler did may have been terrible, but it was hardly unprecedented or unique.

This school of thought, which came to the fore in the 1980s, was thoroughly discredited in the scholarly realm as a generation of younger German historians knocked down its arguments brick by brick. But the *sentiments* continued to find expression elsewhere, particularly in the political arena. Enter Jean Marie Le Pen and Jorg Haider.

According to the Anti-Defamation League of B'nai Brith (ADL), an organization that monitors anti-Semitism around the world, Le Pen, the leader of France's National Front party, is "a right-wing extremist leader...who has a long history of anti-Semitism, racism, and bigotry."[43] Unquestionably, the ADL is right. But the paucity of actual anti-Semitic remarks it was able to dredge from his career—on one occasion he called the Nazi gas chambers "a mere detail" in history, on another he alleged that France's President Jacques Chirac was "in the pay of Jewish organizations," and on still others he has consorted with Holocaust denial—suggests that he is not an anti-Semite of the virulent or obsessive kind.[44] Most of the time, he is an equal-opportunity xenophobe. If he has contempt for the Jews of France, he has contempt for all outsiders, immigrants and others, whom—like the Jews—he deems insufficiently French.

In this respect, Le Pen's appeal is quite similar to that of Haider, the head of Austria's Freedom Party, although Haider emerges more directly from Nazi roots. (His parents had both been active members of the Austrian Nazi Party even before Hitler's rise to power, and his father had joined Hitler Youth as far back as 1929.) Born in 1950, a half-decade after the war, Haider himself profited handsomely from the expropriation and murder of Jews, inheriting from an uncle a huge tract of prime timber and hunting land in Carinthia that had been "Aryanized," i.e., confiscated from its Jewish owners.

Haider has clearly been stamped by this upbringing. He has made a point of speaking at reunions of Waffen SS veterans, and his sympathy for the Nazi past has led him into more explicit flirtations with anti-Semitism. He speaks in veiled language of the American "East Coast" establishment that blackmails Austria into paying reparations for wartime crimes, and minimizes Nazi crimes by describing the death factories as mere "punishment camps."[45] But a central fact about Haider, as of Le Pen, is that anti-Semitism is not the essence of his appeal. Both men have made their mark in politics as xenophobes, and both have found a way to profit politically from the profound social changes in progress in their respective countries.

Indeed, in the effort to gain respectability and electoral support, both Haider and Le Pen have been at pains to distance themselves from prior anti-Semitic stances, emphasizing instead the perils of unchecked immigration and concomitant issues like welfare abuse and crime, while also raising nationalist themes revolving around the dangers of tighter European integration. Haider, in particular, has made a point of stressing the importance of friendship between Austria and the state of Israel, and has made a visit to the Holocaust Memorial Museum in Washington, D.C. Le Pen, for his part, has suggested that French Jews make common cause with him in containing the troubles unleashed by the Arab influx.

On the electoral stage, in any event, the soft anti-Semitism of the European Right appears to have a limited future; the wave ridden by Le Pen and Haider has already moved from crest to trough. In the spring of 2002, Le Pen managed to score a stunning upset in a first round of balloting, forcing the resignation of Prime Minister Lionel Jospin, but in the ensuing runoff he lost to Chirac by the largest landslide in the history of the republic, and at age seventy-three he would seem to have slim prospects for a second comeback. For Jorg Haider, the high-water mark of his Freedom Party came in 1999, when it obtained a stunning 27 percent of the vote. Haider, wrote Roger Cohen of the *New York Times* in the aftermath, "is a possible taste of the future." But the future did not arrive. Mainstream politicians co-opted his nationalist themes, and the "astonishingly broad support" discerned by Cohen evanesced in astonishingly short order.[46] By November 2002, the Freedom Party garnered a mere 10.2 percent of the vote.

If the fortunes of the far Right have fallen, the moderate Right has been no more successful in capitalizing on anti-Semitic sentiments. Not surprisingly, given Germany's tortured past, attitudes toward Jews and the state of Israel remain fraught in that country, with feelings of resentment and even hatred in some sectors mingling with feelings of guilt in others, each intersecting with a pronounced if somewhat artificial strain of philo-Semitism in still others. Among German elites, the taboo on overt expressions of anti-Semitism remains in place: there are limits to what can be said about Jews, as well as restrictions on the kinds of criticisms that can be made of Israel, a state to which Germany has assumed a special relationship. Whenever the taboo is breached, a great deal of public anguish and soul-searching follows.

The bad news about Germany today is that even some mainstream politicians have begun to test the limits. The good news is that the exercise has thus far failed to ignite much interest, let alone enthusiasm, among voters. The most prominent case in point is that of the late Jürgen Möllemann, formerly the deputy chair of the centrist Free Democrat Party (FDP).

The story goes like this: In the summer of 2001, the Free Democrats in North Rhine-Westphalia, where Möllemann was a key figure, accepted a Syrian-born deputy, Jamal Karsli, as a member of their party in the local parliament. Karsli, who had been forced out of the Green Party after complaining about Germany's "Zionist lobby" and accusing its officials of harboring a pro-Israel bias, almost immediately ignited a controversy within the FDP when he charged the government of Israel with engaging in "Nazi methods," a comparison previously deemed out of bounds in public discourse.[47] Möllemann attempted to defend Karsli from his detractors, leading to widespread criticism of the Free Democrats for condoning anti-Semitism in their ranks. In the end, Karsli was forced out of the party.

A year later, in the German federal election campaign, Möllemann made his own carefully plotted foray in the same direction. He began by openly justifying Arab terrorist attacks against Israeli civilians on Israeli territory, declaring of Palestinian violence, "I would resist, too, and use force to do so...not just in my country but in the aggressor's country as well."[48] Even before the ensuing controversy had subsided, Möllemann was in the limelight again, castigating Michel Friedman, vice-president of Germany's Central Council of Jews, for an "intolerant, spiteful manner,"[49] which, he claimed, along with Ariel Sharon's aggressiveness, was "awakening anti-Semitic sentiments" in Germany.[50]

By the unrestrained standards of Western Europe these days, this sounds almost quaint. But in the German context, the attempt to gain political ground by tapping into resentment of Jewish "power" was unprecedented. That the episode occurred at all suggests that at least one respectable politician had calculated there might be profit in the naked baiting of Jews. If so, the calculation proved to be a mistake. Throughout the election season, Möllemann was the target of attacks from across the political spectrum. The FDP's leader, Guido Westerwelle, issued a written statement denying that his party was in any way anti-Semitic. Ultimately he forced Möllemann to resign, though only after the Free Democrats had been pummeled by the voters and shunted to the fringe of the political scene. In today's Germany, it appears that anti-Semitism is not a ticket for electoral success.

❖

Of all the anti-Semitic currents ever to have flowed across Europe, Christian anti-Semitism remains by far the deepest and most powerful. Centuries of teaching—that the Jews refused to recognize Jesus as the Messiah and were instead responsible for his death on the cross at Golgotha, that they bear the mark of Cain and deserve eternal hellfire for the crime—have been absorbed and reabsorbed through the millennial preachments of the major denominations. The result has been the all-too-familiar litany of everyday persecution as well as of much greater horrors extending from the massacres of entire Jewish communities during the Crusades to the climax of European anti-Semitism in the crematoria of the Holocaust. The weight of this past has left an impression that finds expression today in the words of churchmen and congregants alike.

But what form does that expression take? The dominant picture arising from any survey of the major Christian denominations in the postwar era is of institutions grappling with their own culpability for the horrors of European Nazism, and searching, sometimes fitfully, sometimes inadequately, for a way to shed and atone for Christianity's contribution to the catastrophe. In this, the Roman Catholic Church has led the way, but some branches of Protestantism have also taken part, with the Anglican Church being a notable laggard.

For centuries, the Lutheran Church disseminated some of the most toxic ideas in the history of anti-Semitism. It was Martin Luther himself who, in his celebrated pamphlet *Against the Jews and Their Lies,* railed against the chosen people in a tirade perhaps unsurpassed until the Nazi era. Luther followed his imprecations with practical directives, imploring Christians to burn synagogues, confiscate Jewish sacred texts, ban Jews from praying, and compel Jews to engage exclusively in physical labor. Lutherans over the centuries continued to propagate these teachings with varying degrees of fervor.

But in the postwar era, the Lutheran Church, both in the United States and in Europe, has moved (in its own decentralized way) to repudiate the anti-Semitic doctrines that formerly lay at its core. Most recently, the Synod of the Evangelical Lutheran Church in Bavaria, a church at the very heart of Nazi anti-Semitism, promulgated a "basic statement" disavowing any form of "anti-Judaism." Like other documents in this genre, it contains some naked equivocations and striking half-tones—did the synod really have to wait fifty years after the Holocaust to proclaim that "defamatory remarks against Jews and Judaism should be *avoided*" (emphasis added)? Nevertheless, the statement goes far in a new direction, declaring that the church formally "disassociates itself from Martin Luther's anti-Semitic writings and remarks" and explicitly acknowledging the church's complicity in the mass murder of Jews.[51]

❖

The shift under way in Lutheranism—the Bavarian synod is among the last branches of the church to act—finds a close parallel in Catholicism. The first major milestone came in 1962 when Pope John XXIII convened the Second Vatican Council to push for, among other things, a radical alteration of Church teaching concerning Jews. Although John died before the council completed its deliberations, under his successor, Paul VI, the Vatican promulgated *Nostra Aetate: A Declaration on the Relationship of the Church to Non-Christian Religions*. Although leaving intact the historicity of the charge of deicide, the declaration abandoned the Augustinian view that the Jews shall forever bear the burden for the crime of their forebears:

> What happened in [Christ's] passion cannot be charged against all Jews, without distinction, then alive, nor against the Jews of today. Although the Church is the new People of God, the Jews should not be represented as rejected by God or accursed, as if this followed from Holy Scriptures.

Nostra Aetate likewise noted that Catholics share a common patrimony with the Jews and are under a positive obligation to decry "hatred, persecutions, displays of anti-Semitism, directed against Jews at any time and by anyone."[52]

The foundation built in this historic document has been

strengthened in our own time by Pope John Paul II, who as a young man in Poland was an eyewitness to the bloodiest horrors of Nazism and who, in 1986, became the first pope to set foot in a synagogue, possibly since the earliest days of the Church. Whereas Paul VI had studiously avoided even uttering the name of the state of Israel during his visit to the Holy Land in 1963, John Paul II broke decisively with precedent and moved in 1993 to establish diplomatic relations between the Holy See and the Jewish state. Traveling to Jerusalem in 2000, he visited the Holocaust memorial Yad Vashem and issued a ringing denunciation of Christian anti-Semitism, declaring himself "deeply saddened by the hatred, acts of persecution, and displays of anti-Semitism directed against the Jews by Christians at any time and in any place."[53]

In 1998, John Paul II oversaw the publication of *We Remember: A Reflection on the Shoah*. This document represents the fullest attempt by the Church to examine the relationship between Catholic teachings and the "indelible stain" that was the Holocaust. Briefly reviewing the long history of Christian anti-Semitism, the document frankly acknowledges that sentiments of "anti-Judaism" prevalent "in some Christian quarters" led not only to "generalized discrimination" but also to "expulsions," "attempts at forced conversions," and "violence, looting, even massacres."[54]

There is room to object to a number of points in the statement. For example, the Vatican's hard distinction between Christian "anti-Judaism" and the modern, Nazi brand of "anti-Semitism" is not as crystalline as *We Remember* suggests. Again, while rightly pointing to the heroic Christian individuals who undertook acts of astonishing bravery on behalf of Jews during the Holocaust, *We Remember* entirely evades the role of the many other Christians, including many Catholics, who not only failed to resist but played an active and approving part in the unfolding Nazi horror. Thus, elements of the German Catholic Church actively cooperated with Nazi authorities, carrying out their murderous program or issuing statements avidly supportive of Hitler and his war aims.

We Remember apart, a number of more recent Vatican actions have raised disturbing questions of their own. Thus, a joint Jewish-Catholic commission set up to review Vatican archives pertaining to the Holocaust collapsed in 2001 amid charges leveled by a high Vatican official that its Jewish members had a "clear propagandistic goal to damage the Holy See" and were engaged in a "slanderous campaign" against the Church; even some Catholic scholars were appalled by this unfounded accusation.[55] Other disquieting episodes have included the Vatican's canonization of the Polish Catholic priest Maximillian Kolbe, an anti-Nazi resister but also a confirmed anti-Semite; the planting of a large cross at Auschwitz, which appropriated to Christianity the site of the mass murder of millions of Jews; and a series of articles by Vatican-sponsored publications unremittingly hostile to the state of Israel.

None of this is to take away from the larger story of the Catholic Church and other major branches of Christianity over the past fifty years, which is that of institutions engaged in a genuine and sincere effort to reconceive their relationship with the Jewish people. But this effort evidently is still fragmentary, occasionally incoherent, and subject to the vicissitudes of the moment. In particular, the recent upsurge in anti-Semitism has enlisted the enthusiasm of a number of churchmen, while others, vocal in denouncing the anti-Jewish bigotry of the past, have been utterly silent in the face of the anti-Jewish bigotry—and worse, anti-Jewish violence—of the present.

A reflexive hatred of Israel now appears to be rife within the Anglican Church in Great Britain. "Whenever I print anything sympathetic to Israel," sighs the editor of the church's official newspaper, "I get deluged with complaints that I am Zionist and racist."[56] In Denmark, a Lutheran bishop in Copenhagen has likened Ariel Sharon to the biblical King Herod, who ordered the death of all male children in Bethlehem under the age of two. In Italy, the liberal daily *La Stampa* has resurrected the oldest Christian anti-Semitic canard of all: a cartoon depicted the infant Jesus looking up from his manger at an Israeli tank and pleading, "Don't tell me they want to kill me again."[57] From the Vatican, indifference to the murder of Jews in Israel is coupled with the charge by some that the Jews themselves are committing genocide. "Indescribable barbarity" was the phrase used by Franciscan officials in Rome describing Israel's attempt to arrest Palestinian terrorists who had taken shelter in the Church of the Nativity in Bethlehem.[58] In the hallowed "land of Jesus," complained the Vatican daily *L'Osservatore Romano,* Israel was exhibiting an "irritating haughtiness" and engaging in "aggression which becomes extermination."[59] One could easily adduce many more such examples, not only from Western churches but in Eastern Orthodoxy as well.

❖

Still, it is neither the political anti-Semitism of the European Right nor the theological anti-Semitism of organized Christianity that one can honestly point to and say, here is where the new hatred of Jews has its inspiration and takes its motive force. Even if they were more single-minded in their attitudes toward the Jews than the evidence indicates, neither the Right nor organized Christianity mobilizes the power it once did in Europe. No, one must look to another native European tradition, with a pedigree that goes back to the very beginnings of the French Enlightenment. This is the anti-Semitism of the "progressives," whose home is in the middle of the respectable establishment and on the Left.

This strain of anti-Semitism loathes the Jews not on explicitly racialist or on religious grounds but on "universalist" ones. Its ignoble history runs from Voltaire (who regarded the Jews as "the most abominable people in the world"), through Karl Marx (to whom Polish Jews were the "filthiest of all races"), then seven decades of Soviet Communism with its flagrantly anti-Israel foreign policy and its harshly oppressive attitude toward Soviet Jewish citizens, then the 1960s New Left, the homegrown German and Italian terrorism of recent decades, and the alignment of progressive European opinion with the cause of Palestinian "liberation." Today, a new chapter is being written. Among those burning the Star of David and chanting obscene slogans against the Jewish state in the streets of Europe, there are surely some neo-Nazis, but a greater host of environmentalists, pacifists, anarchists, antiglobalists and socialists.

A cacophony of themes can be heard from Europe's Left today. Some of it is a kind of seepage of the virulent propaganda that emerges from the printing presses of the Islamic world. In France, for example, there is *The Horrifying Fraud,* a book by Thierry Meyssan, a researcher who heads an organization called, aptly enough, the Voltaire Network. Meyssan contends that the terrorism of September 11 was not organized by Osama bin Laden and al-Qaeda, but rather was the work of a right-wing conspiracy within the Pentagon. In his book, Meyssan avoids the variant of this theory that is widely accepted within the Arab world—namely, that Israel's intelligence agency, the Mossad, was behind the attacks. But in interviews, he has been less discreet. "Six months before the event, Israeli intelligence services had warned the Americans" about the impending attack, Meyssan told an Iranian journalist. "Two hours before the incidents," he added, "an Israeli telecommunications company left a message on the mobile phones of everyone living in the vicinity of the World Trade Center buildings and warned them of what was about to happen."[60] Though *The Horrifying Fraud* was widely ridiculed in the French media, this didn't prevent it from becoming a runaway bestseller.

Anti-Semitic agitprop for children, of the "progressive" variety, is also in wide circulation. Flammarion, one of France's most prestigious publishing houses, has brought out *Dreaming of Palestine,* a novel written by a fifteen-year-old girl, an Arab resident of Italy, about a violent confrontation between a group of Palestinian teenagers and the Israel Defense Force. The Jews who appear in this children's book are insatiable bloodletters, willing to rape women and murder children with Nazi-like enthusiasm:

When they were still small children, Jihad and Riham's parents and their four-month-old twins were exterminated. One day tanks had entered the village and the soldiers had fired on everyone around, women, old people, children. They entered all the houses, they set some alight with the families still inside, in others they raped the women, stole the money, and destroyed everything.

Facing this pitiless adversary, the children come to conclude that they have an obligation to "kill all the Israelis"; the preferred method is suicide bombings. When one of the teenage heroes sacrifices himself to murder five Israeli soldiers, his friends eulogize him, although they deplore his ineffectualness: "You are brave, Gamal, we'll miss you.... But why blow up your life to kill only five soldiers? You could have killed hundreds of them."[61]

Dreaming of Palestine has been widely acclaimed. A critic for French National Radio called the work "surprisingly mature…a novel [imbued] with what makes the great texts: suffering and hope."[62] Complaints by French Jewish organizations did induce Flammarion to provide "balance" by issuing another title with an entirely different slant: *Anna's Suitcase,* a story about a teenage Jewish girl who meets her fate at the hands of the Nazis. But there was no rush on French bookstores for *Anna's Suitcase.* On the other hand, sales of *Dreaming of Palestine* outstripped any other book of its genre published in recent years.

The mind of the French reading public is hardly a *tabula rasa.* France's major newspapers—*Le Monde* foremost among them—consistently treat Israel as an aggressive pariah that tramples on the rights of innocent Palestinian civilians without any cause save a fanatical devotion to acquiring settlements and seizing Arab land. French television news presents an endless parade of Palestinian victims of Israeli aggression: men humiliated at Israeli checkpoints on the West Bank, women clutching bloodied babies as they flee in terror from their homes, children shot and dying in the alleys of wretched refugee camps. Almost wholly missing is any context for the violence—which instead is made to appear as though it stemmed entirely from the Israeli side—let alone a comparable parade of Jewish victims of Palestinian suicide bombings.

Such a perspective is by no means confined to France. In Holland, the well-connected Gretta Duisenberg—whose husband, Wim, is the president of the European Central Bank, and who was herself selected by a leading Dutch daily in 2002 as "Amsterdamer of the year"— founded an anti-Israel organization called "Stop the Occupation." Busy collecting signatures for a petition against Israeli "imperialism," she joked to a news reporter that her objective was to gather "six million" names. In Madame Duisenberg's view, "Israeli occupation of the Palestinian territories is worse than the Nazi occupation of the Netherlands."[63]

In Norway, the Nobel committee conferred its 1994 peace prize on Yitzhak Rabin, Shimon Peres and Yasir Arafat. At the time, one honest member of the committee, Kara Christiansen, resigned in protest, rightly calling Arafat a terrorist unworthy of the award.[64] More recently, however, other committee members, one of them a Lutheran bishop, have attempted to strip not Arafat but Shimon Peres of the prize. His crime: participating in a government that has violated the "intention and spirit" of the award. Meanwhile, a visitor to Norway's parliament wearing a Star of David on his chest pocket to express solidarity with the state of Israel was accosted by guards and ordered to remove his jacket—although the halls of the parliament building are regularly filled with visitors sporting pro-Palestinian symbols on their clothes and kefiyas on their heads.

In Great Britain, the idea of Israel as a homeland for the Jewish people has been called "a load of crap" by Claire Rayner, president of the British Humanist Association. By contrast, she defends the suicide bombings of Israeli restaurants and buses as both understandable and justifiable: "If you treat a group of people the way Palestinians have been treated they will use the only weapon they have, which is their individual lives."[65] More established figures in England voice sentiments fully as bizarre and, if anything, more venomous. Tom Paulin is a professor at Oxford, an arts commentator for the British Broadcasting Corporation and a poet whose recent verse includes a lament for a small Palestinian boy "gunned down by the Zionist SS." "I never believed that Israel had the right to exist at all," Paulin told the Egyptian weekly *Al-Ahram* in April, and Jews from Brooklyn who have settled in the West Bank "are Nazis, racists.... They should be shot dead."

To a critic for the *Observer,* Paulin is that "rare thing in contemporary British culture, 'the writer as conscience.'"[66] Many others seem to agree. The *Irish Times* found Paulin "a rigorous respecter of language" who "does not dilute his words."[67] The highly regarded British novelist and biographer A. N. Wilson (who has also "reluctantly" proclaimed that the state of Israel no longer has a right to exist) has called Paulin a "brilliant scholar and literary critic" and reminded us that "many in [England] and throughout the world would echo his views on the tragic events in the Middle East."[68] On this last point, Wilson is correct.

One could devote pages to the malevolent mythmaking of the mainstream British and European press in reporting on the "slaughter" of Palestinians in the battle of Jenin in the spring of 2002. There, according to the *Evening Standard* of London, the Israelis aimed for "the near-total destruction of the lives and livelihoods of the camp's 15,000 inhabitants."[69] In the view of A. N. Wilson, writing in the same newspaper, "We are talking here of massacre, and a cover-up, of genocide."[70] To the *Guardian,* Jenin was a "crime of especial notoriety" and "every bit as repellent" as Osama bin Laden's attack on New York on September 11.[71] Reported the correspondent for the London *Times,* "Rarely in more than a decade of war reporting from Bosnia, Chechnya, Sierra Leone, Kosovo, have I seen such deliberate destruction, such disrespect for human life."[72]

What one would not have grasped from reading the British press was that Israel, in rooting out the terrorists who had illegally placed themselves amid civilians in the Jenin refugee camp, had eschewed the use of air power, which was

permitted under international law. Rather, in an effort to minimize civilian Palestinian casualties, and at great risk to its own
men, the Israeli military sent in reservists on foot. As a result—
though the British press suggested that thousands of
Palestinians had perished, and though the United Nations
envoy, Terje Roed-Larsen, gave official sanction to those
estimates without undertaking an inquiry—subsequent investigation revealed a total of fifty-two Palestinian deaths in the
battle, mainly of guerrilla fighters, while the IDF lost twenty-
three soldiers of its own in this costly determination to conduct
itself in the most humane fashion possible.

❖

The *Economist,* Great Britain's influential newsweekly, has
played a special role in piling obloquy on the Jewish state.
Emphasizing the suffering of the Palestinians at the hands of
the "brutal" Israelis, the magazine has downplayed the violence
inflicted on Israeli civilians by Palestinian suicide bombers and
has largely passed over in silence the murderous incitement
that is the daily fare of the Palestinian media. "In the razed
heart of the Jenin refugee camp," the *Economist* intoned at the
time of the Israeli incursion, "Palestinians were shoveling out
their decomposed dead…. The danger of epidemic is real." It
continued, "Like earthquake victims, the Palestinians in Jenin,
Nablus, and elsewhere in the West Bank need massive human-
itarian help"—help that "is hindered by the Israeli army's
sieges." As Bret Stephens of the *Jerusalem Post* noted, the
Economist subsequently declined to report that no epidemic
had materialized, nor did it describe for its readers the terrorist
tactics employed by Palestinian guerrillas, including the use of
ambulances to ferry explosives across army checkpoints into
Israel. Instead, it resurrected a time-honored anti-Semitic
canard about, of all things, Jewish avarice! "Israel is a superior
country," it editorialized with a smirk. "But it has to abate its
greed for other people's land."73

The *Economist* represents the liberal establishment, as
does the British Broadcasting Corporation (BBC), which uses

television transmissions worldwide to paint an utterly lopsided picture in which the Jewish state's most dangerous enemies are presented as well-intended gentlemen and the Israelis themselves as demons. Israel's prime minister, Ariel Sharon, is regularly characterized by the BBC as a "hardliner," a warmongering retired general who "led punitive military operations," launched a "disastrous invasion of Lebanon," favors "harsh occupation measures," and believes that "the end justifies the means." And those bent on Israel's destruction? Sheikh Ahmed Yassin, one of the top leaders of the fundamentalist Islamic terror organization Hamas, is typically identified by the BBC as Hamas's "spiritual figurehead" and "the moderate face of the Palestinian Islamists." The worst it can find to say of him is that he occasionally lapses into "fiery" speech; seldom if ever has it mentioned that by his own word, he intends to remove the Jewish state from the map and drive its residents into the sea.[74]

The British media have been in the vanguard of the assault on Israel, but British universities have not lagged far behind. At campus anti-Israel demonstrations, "death to the Jews" has been among the obscene slogans to be heard, while to be seen are banners with swastikas superimposed over Stars of David. At London University's School of Oriental and African Studies, Jewish students have been subjected to harassment, while inflammatory lectures are offered with titles like, "Sharon: A New Hitler for a New Age." In certain shops in Oxford, books by Israelis are banned.

British universities also gave birth to a widely circulated petition calling for a moratorium on grants by European educational institutions to any and all Israeli scholars and researchers. Under this proposal, Israelis were to be punished simply for their status as citizens of the Jewish state. Silent about the remorseless terrorism against Israeli civilians, the petition denounced Israel's government as "impervious to moral appeals."[75] Among the hundreds of signers of this meretricious document were scholars from institutions of higher learning in virtually every country of Europe, including the famed British Darwinist, Richard Dawkins.

Some British academics, not content with merely circulating such ideas, have begun to put them into practice. An Israeli seeking a doctoral fellowship at Oxford received a rejection letter from the head of one of the university's research laboratories. "No way would I take on somebody who had served in the Israeli army," it read. "As you may be aware, I am not the only UK scientist with these views."[76] The professors running two scholarly publications on translation, both ostensibly devoted to promoting cross-cultural understanding, acted to remove academics from their scholarly boards entirely on the basis of Israeli citizenship. One of those let go was a world-renowned linguist, who also happened to be the former director of Israel's Amnesty International chapter and an outspoken critic of Israeli policies toward Palestinians. But never mind; to the editor of the *Translator,* she was, as a Jewish citizen of a Jewish state, ipso facto an agent of aggression against the Palestinians. It goes without saying that no academic from any other country around the world, no matter how barbaric its human rights record, has been treated in an equivalent manner. To cap it all, the editor behind the sacking insisted, "I am most definitely not anti-Semitic, anti-Jewish, or even anti-Israeli as such."[77]

❖

If the main dish of the European Left has been fanatical agitation against Israel, it often comes with trimmings that betray the influence of other European traditions of anti-Semitism. Henrik Bachner, a researcher at Lund University in Sweden, has described how the process works in his own homeland. In the late 1960s and early 1970s, he writes, radical anti-Zionist ideas were injected into the Swedish body politic by fringe Marxist and left-wing Christian groups and gradually came to exercise a broad impact on the mainstream establishment. These ideas, once they achieved a "measure of respectability," had the additional effect of "weakening the taboo on anti-Semitism to the point where anti-Jewish sentiments surfaced within the mainstream political culture, not least within the media."

92

These anti-Semitic (as opposed to strictly anti-Israel) sentiments often took the form of "age-old Christian anti-Jewish
perceptions...woven into—and rationalized as—criticism of
Israeli government policies."[78]

Some examples: After Israel's incursion into Lebanon in
1982, one columnist for a respectable Swedish newspaper saw
fit to chastise Israel for being in the grip of "Old Testament ideology," which led him to doubt whether "there can be peace
before this unyielding grip has loosened."[79] Another newspaper emphasized that Judaism "is a particularly warlike and
murderous teaching or 'religion.' ...Accordingly, the expansionist global and genocidal policy Israel pursues...is totally
supported by the holy scripture of Judaism, the Old Testament."[80] Other papers have focused on Jewish "chosenness,"
condemning the massacres committed by "God's elect nation"
and noting that "the war policy of the Israeli government finds
support in the Bible." Still others have connected Jewish chosenness with Jewish manipulation and greed. Here is an item
from the newspaper *Västgöta-Demokraten:*

> If one believes the old source texts, Israel was God's chosen
> people. It is therefore perhaps not a difficult choice for such a
> people, using all the means at its disposal, especially military
> options, to strive to extend its chosen property and territory....
> Jews and pawnbrokers used to be virtually synonymous con-
> cepts, but things have moved on and they now invest their
> assets in the West Bank, which pays a higher dividend....
> We need to differentiate between Christianity and Judaism—
> the Jews follow the law of Moses, a specially composed story,
> particularly well suited to military and warlike adventures.[81]

❖

Along with Christian themes, the European Left has begun to
draw on some of the more entrenched right-wing anti-Semitic
myths, with direct and indirect echoes of the notorious *Protocols of the Elders of Zion*. A particularly commonplace notion
these days is that Jews are operating behind the scenes to
manipulate world events for self-interested and nefarious ends.
On the eve of the war with Iraq in late 2002 and early 2003,

even in the most enlightened circles of the European Left and in the high seats of government, there were those who explained that the coming battle was not about oil nor about Saddam Hussein's weapons of mass destruction; rather, Washington was being conned by supporters of the state of Israel around the world, and especially by American Jews.

For example, Rudolph Scharping, a former German defense minister who served for a time in Chancellor Gerhard Schroeder's cabinet, declared (according to a paraphrased summary by the columnist William Safire) that "Bush was motivated to overthrow Saddam by his need to curry favor with... 'a powerful—perhaps overly powerful—Jewish lobby' in the coming U.S. elections."[82]*

In Great Britain, the same idea was put more emphatically. "The foreign policy of the world's only global power," said one magazine article, "is being made by a small clique that is unrepresentative of either the U.S. population or the mainstream foreign-policy establishment." This "clique," it was explained, is composed largely of Jewish-American "neoconservatives" who "took over Washington and steered the U.S. into a Middle Eastern war unrelated to any plausible threat to the U.S. and opposed by the public of every country in the world except Israel."[83] The BBC chimed in with a special two-part installment of its news magazine, *Panorama,* devoted to the immense power of the "Jewish lobby" and the especially insidious role played by Jewish "neoconservatives" strategically placed throughout the highest levels of the Bush administration. The existence of these organized forces supposedly accounts for the otherwise inexplicable American support for Israel despite its rapacious treatment of the Palestinians.

What the pundits write and the televisions trumpet, the politicians inevitably echo. In Great Britain it was not long before even members of Parliament were espousing similar the-

---

*After Scharping's remarks were cited by Safire, the former German defense minister issued a denial. Safire stood by his reporting. *New York Times,* September 19, 2002.

ories. In the wake of the Iraq war, Tam Dalyell, a longtime Labor MP, accused Prime Minister Tony Blair of being "unduly influenced by a cabal of Jewish advisers." Dalyell pointed in particular to Lord Levy, Blair's personal envoy to the Middle East; to his fellow MP Peter Mandelson; and to Foreign Minister Jack Straw, all of whom had supported Britain's alliance with the United States against Saddam and were thought to be favoring further action against Syria and Iran. "I am not going to be labeled anti-Semitic," said Dalyell in defense of his remarks; "my children worked on a kibbutz." Nevertheless, he went on, when it comes to the Jewish role in British affairs, "one has to be candid."[84]

Public reaction to the Dalyell flap was as instructive as the episode itself. A slew of commentators rushed to point out that neither Mandelson nor Straw could be considered Jewish, except, of course, under the notorious Nuremberg Laws of Nazi Germany. Dalyell himself was charged by some with being anti-Semitic. But almost all of these critics were Jewish. As for officials of the Labor Party, they maintained a discreet silence or treated the matter as the errant intervention of a sometimes wayward politician.

The Dalyell affair was not anomalous, though. "Too frequently to discount now, I hear remarks that the Jews are to blame for everything," noted the writer Petronella Wyatt in the London *Spectator* in late 2001. There she recounted how one of her acquaintances, a man whom she described as "intelligent [and] well-meaning," inquired of her in full seriousness: "As a journalist, do you think there is an international Jewish conspiracy?" And from someone else in her circle, a life peer active in the cause of human rights, came the declamation: "Well, the Jews have been asking for it, and now, thank God, we can say what we think at last." From an abundance of comments like these, Wyatt concluded that "since 11 September, anti-Semitism and its open expression [have] become respectable once more." This, she added, was true not only "in Germany or Catholic central Europe—but at London dinner tables."[85]

In attendance at one dinner party widely reported in the

British press was Daniel Bernard, the French ambassador to the Court of St. James. In the course of the evening Bernard politely told the assembled guests that "the current troubles in the world were all because of 'that shitty little country Israel.'" And he asked, "'Why should the world be in danger of World War III because of *those* people?'"[86] In addition to Bernard, who claimed to have misspoken when his remarks appeared in the press, there was also the case of Lady Powell, one of the glossier fixtures on the London social-political scene. At a London luncheon, she reportedly explained that she could not bear the Jews and asserted that "everything that was happening to them was their own fault." When the remark was received with a shocked silence, she remonstrated, "Oh come on, you all feel like that."[87]*

❖

A considerable literature has been devoted to plumbing the nature of Europe's millennial "Jewish problem," and the current flare-up has already given rise to a fresh round of theorizing about its root causes, old and new. Among all the competing explanations, there is one that demands emphasis, not because it is the most significant but because it is in some ways the most perverse. Among many Europeans, there appears to be a deep-seated psychological need to lighten the burden of guilt for the Holocaust by defaming its victims posthumously. And this points to an extraordinary paradox. For if memory of the Holocaust has served in some sense to undercut the old anti-Semitism of the European Right, it may well be fueling the new anti-Semitism of the Left.

In the first decades after World War II, the Nazi genocide was perceived in Europe as a specifically Jewish tragedy. Although the war unleashed by Hitler had claimed millions of non-Jewish lives, it was widely recognized that his singular

---

*When these remarks surfaced in the media, Lady Powell denied ever having uttered them.

innovation—death camps designed to exterminate millions in a factory-style operation—was the instrument of a genocide directed exclusively against the Jewish people, the only group the German dictator attempted to annihilate in its entirety as his wars of conquest were in progress.

But in recent years this plain understanding of the Nazi genocide has been inverted. The Jews are today perceived, in the words of the French analyst Michel Gurfinkiel, as "only 'accidentally' the victims of Nazism," just another minority group in the long history of minority groups who have suffered at the hands of intolerant majorities.[88] Nazism, in turn, has been cast less as an anti-Semitic movement than as a generally racist one.

The 2000 Stockholm International Forum on the Holocaust was perhaps the largest single global conference ever devoted to memorializing the extermination of European Jewry, a gathering attended and addressed by European heads of state. At this general convocation, more than a few of the speakers described the victims of the concentration camps as fellow "Europeans" or as fellow "human beings," or simply as innocent "men, women, and children"—while scrupulously avoiding the term "Jews." The Holocaust, in short, is being universalized; its particular Jewish nature is being erased as it is enlisted in the service of a variety of contemporary causes, including preeminently the antiracism campaigns so fashionable today in a Europe grappling with a large immigrant influx from Africa and the Arab world.

Nor does the perversity stop there; universalization is only the first step. The "antiracism" movement, however noble it sounds in theory, proceeds to twist the very concept of racial prejudice in such a way as to suggest that Jews, having once been its victims, now merit the world's censure as its perpetrators. This too is not exactly a new theme, although it has lately been taken to extremes of demonization. Visiting the Anne Frank House in Amsterdam in the late 1970s, Gurfinkiel noted "a wall bearing premonitory messages about 'new Holocausts in the making.'" One of these messages "warned darkly of the consequences of the electoral victory in Israel…of 'Menachem Begin's far-Right Likud party.'"[89]

Throughout the Islamic world, as we saw earlier, the history and symbols of the Holocaust have been wielded as instruments of propaganda against the state of Israel. Like much of Islamic anti-Semitism itself, this staple was not indigenous, having been incubated in the rhetorical laboratories of the Soviet Union and long ago adopted by the most respectable spokesmen of the European Left. Olaf Palme, a former prime minister of Sweden and the leader of his country's Social Democratic Party, was drawing parallels between the fate of the Jews in the Holocaust at the hands of the Nazis and the fate of the Palestinians at the hands of the Israelis as far back as the early 1980s. On one occasion, he spoke of remembering the fate of "Jewish children in concentration camps and ghettos and realizing the terrible crime that had been committed against them"—the same terrible crime, he added, that came to mind "when we see pictures of Palestinian children, persecuted in exactly the same way." Today, according to Palme, by means of "an extraordinary reversal of roles…it is the Palestinians, not the Jews, who are being persecuted and are threatened by 'liquidation.' …Today it is the Palestinians who are locked up in a new Warsaw Ghetto."[90]

There has in fact been an "extraordinary reversal," but not the one that Palme described. It consists of the breathtaking way in which the victims of Nazism have been transformed into Nazis themselves by a distortion that is every bit as distant from historical reality, and every bit as slanderous of Jewish memory, as the work of Holocaust deniers like David Irving. But comparisons that were a shocking novelty when introduced by Olaf Palme two decades ago, and that were ignored when mouthed repeatedly by Muslims and Arabs, have ricocheted back into polite, liberal European society and have now become commonplace. The Oxford poet Tom Paulin writes of the "Zionist SS" and his celebrity status grows. In the pages of the Belgian newspaper *Le Soir,* Simon-Pierre Nothomb, a descendant of one of his country's leading families, informs readers that the West Bank, "like Poland during its dark years, is dotted with concentration camps," while in the Gaza Strip, "as in 1941 Warsaw, the local authorities are ordered to hand over their subjects forthwith, according to lists compiled by the occupying authorities."[91] This is a popular theme: Oona King, a Labor member of the British Parliament of African-American and Jewish parentage, is on record saying that her fellow Jews, "in escaping the ashes of the Holocaust...have incarcerated another people in a hell similar in its nature—though not its extent—to the Warsaw Ghetto."[92] At demonstrations organized by Muslims and German leftists, noted a shrewd columnist for the influential German newspaper *Süddeutsche Zeitung,* one hears "the very slogans that used to get neo-Nazi marches banned...'Jewish pigs,' 'Sieg Heil' and so forth."[93]

An extraordinary inversion of both fact and morality is represented in this spectacle, compelling one to wonder about the motives, the dark psychic purposes it serves. To that same columnist, speculating on how "the hatred of Jews has [become] as socially acceptable...as it is today," the wild anti-Jewish slogans are signs of what Freudians would call a return of the repressed. Among Europeans, he writes, and especially among Germans, there is "a tendency to use the Near East conflict for the purpose of conquering *our own past.... *[I]t used to be that Israel was spared criticism. Today, criticism is heaped on Israel. Because many people believe the [European] past has been conquered, 'the Jews' can once again be held, powerfully, to blame" (emphasis added).[94]

If this analysis is correct—and I think there is much to recommend it—then Europe's most advanced "progressives" are now agents of the most reactionary, and most incendiary, aspects of the past. To the Portuguese novelist José Saramago, Israel is Jewish diabolism writ large. The Israelis, he wrote in the leading Spanish newspaper *El Pais,* echoing classic anti-Semitic language, are motivated by the "monstrous and rooted 'certitude'" that they are "chosen by God" and are in the grip of an "obsessive, psychological and pathologically exclusivist racism." This is what gives them license to exercise their hatred for others, a hatred that is then rationalized and justified by what they endured in the Holocaust. While themselves committing crimes "comparable to Auschwitz," Saramago writes, the Jews "endlessly scratch their own wound to keep it bleeding, to make it incurable, and they show it to the world as if it were a banner."[95]

A crackpot writing to mobilize the inchoate fears and bigotries of other crackpots? One might think so from the lurid imagery, the boiling resentment, the crazed determination to purge, once and for all, a festering guilt. But José Saramago is a leading man of letters, a Nobel laureate in literature. That such words should burst from his lips tells us that a line has been crossed and we have reached a new stage.

We are far from the boundless terrors of World War II—this goes without saying. But that benchmark sets a standard of horror so high that if one relies upon it today for reassurance, all signposts of impending danger are lost. The signals of warning are, however, already abundant enough. "The thought goes before the deed, as the lightning precedes the thunder," wrote Heinrich Heine a century and a half ago. In Europe today we are again seeing the lightning, and we are beginning to hear the claps of thunder.

❖

FOUR

THE END OF THE
AMERICAN EXCEPTION?

W hat of the United States? Can the disease spread here? Has it already?

The history of the United States has been blessedly free of the curses that turned Europe into a vast abattoir. Whatever challenges and difficulties the Jews were to encounter in their new land, they were never the most reviled stratum of society. Even apart from the blacks who were brought here against their will, other immigrant groups, notably Italian and Irish Catholics, were more looked down upon than Jews throughout most of the nineteenth century.

To be sure, anti-Jewish prejudice and discrimination were much in evidence in that era, and in the twentieth century, modern forms of anti-Semitism certainly reared their head. The early decades saw, for example, Henry Ford's crusade in the pages of the newspaper he owned, the *Dearborn Independent,* where he republished the fraudulent *Protocols of the Elders of Zion* and embellished them for the domestic context, explaining that the "United States, because of its tolerance, is a promising field" for Jews to exercise their untoward powers of manipulation and revenge.[1]

Ford's campaign burned out quite rapidly. Within a year or two, his denunciations of world Jewry in the pages of the *Independent* noticeably diminished, and by 1927 he reversed himself entirely, declaring, "I consider it my duty as an honorable man to make amends for the harm I have done to the Jews."[2] But the rise of Nazism in the 1930s brought another and far more intense wave of hatred, whose most notorious spokesman was Charles E. Coughlin, a Roman Catholic priest. Like Ford, Father Coughlin reprinted the *Protocols* in his publication *Social Justice;* on the eve of World War II, his openly anti-Semitic radio broadcasts reached an audience of millions, while organizations allied with his cause, such as the Christian Front, launched boycotts of Jewish merchants.

This burgeoning movement received a powerful boost from the hero Charles Lindbergh, who, having become a prominent isolationist and a leading figure in the America First Committee, described the Jews as a sinister force pushing the U.S. into war. Nevertheless, when war did arrive in the surprise attack on Pearl Harbor, the America First Committee and the anti-Semitic movements in and around it entered a serious decline from which they did not recover. In all, only the palest shadow of a Nazi-style anti-Semitism had darkened U.S. shores, though Americans did display lesser forms of prejudice, and to a surprisingly high degree, even as late as 1945.

In the postwar years, the horrifying revelations from Europe combined with the steady assimilation of American Jewry and a growing, society-wide repugnance for intolerance would ensure that little remained of institutionalized anti-Semitism. True, Jews were kept out of country clubs, their numbers were restricted at universities by quotas, and they were barred from executive suites by more subtle practices. True, also, right-wing fringe groups like the American Nazi Party, the National Renaissance Party and the like continued to agitate against them and especially against their alleged affinity for Communism. But it is significant that Senator Joseph McCarthy, even in his most excessive moments, never acquired an anti-Semitic tinge in his zeal to weed out hidden enemies of the United States, real or imagined.

This, indeed, has been the American rule in the last half-century: the rule of the exception, as we might call it. In the realm of anti-Semitism, as in so many other spheres, America is gratifyingly different. Though we might pause to note certain dark clouds occasionally floating across the horizon, especially in connection with the left-wing radicalism that came to the fore in the late 1960s and 1970s, it makes sense to skip forward to the present day and treat those clouds retrospectively. They cast interesting shadows on our current moment.

❖

In certain ways, and in highly attenuated form, North America today may be starting to resemble Europe. To begin with, there are new elements in the American demographic equation, of which the most significant is the growing number of Muslims. Reliable numbers are hard to come by: a U.S. Department of State fact sheet offers a figure of six million, which is almost certainly much too high, while other estimates range from two to four million. But there is no disagreement that the Muslim population has increased dramatically in recent decades, and that a sizable fraction of that increase is attributable to immigration from the Middle East. According to the Center for Immigration Studies, a Washington D.C. think tank, the influx of immigrants from the Middle East, once mainly Christian Arabs but now mainly Muslims, grew nearly eightfold from 1970 to 2000 and is projected to double again by the end of this decade.

The effect on Jewish security in the United States is already palpable. If physical attacks on Jews and Jewish institutions once came mostly from right-wing or nativist groups, now they come increasingly from Arab militants. We have already noted the hatred of Jews that motivated the organizers and executors of the two plots to topple the Word Trade Center, as well as the (thwarted) attacks on New York's bridges and tunnels. But these highly organized conspiracies are only the best-known dimension of the problem.

In recent years, a growing number of Muslim immigrants have come to serve, in effect, as freelance terrorists. Not directly connected or subservient to any terrorist organization or cell, they are nevertheless steeped in the culture of hatred

that pervades the Middle East, and have taken it upon themselves to carry out violent, semi-spontaneous terrorist attacks
against Jewish (or presumed Jewish) targets.

There has been a series of such outrages. On March 1,
1994, Rashid Baz, a Muslim immigrant from Lebanon, sprayed
a van traversing the Brooklyn Bridge with gunfire. His target
was a group of fifteen Hasidic students. He killed one, Ari Hal-
berstam, age sixteen, and seriously injured three others. The
gunman's motives were said to be "concern" about events in
the Middle East, but both ABC and the *New York Daily News*
reported that he was connected to the Shiite Muslim guerrilla
group Hizbollah. Whatever his precise affiliations, the milieu
from which he (and the two accomplices who helped him hide
his weapons) emerged is no secret. As the *Boston Globe* paraphrased the comments of one Arab resident of Brooklyn, "the
recent surge in violence [against Jews] may be attributed to the
increased militancy among the young men who are now arriv-
ing from the Middle East. They are different, he said, from
those who immigrated a decade ago, like himself."[3]

There is also the case of Ali Abu Kamal, a sixty-nine-year-
old English teacher from Gaza who on February 24, 1997,
ascended to the eighty-sixth floor of the Empire State Building
carrying a .380 caliber Beretta semi-automatic and opened fire
on visitors in the observation tower, injuring six people and
killing one before taking his own life. Although officials
attempted to portray him as a deranged man, the gunman's
two-page suicide note suggested a strong element of "rational-
ity," Middle Eastern style, in his conduct. The note, entitled
"Charter of Honour," listed a series of "bitter enemies" who
"must be annihilated and exterminated." Among them were
the "Zionists." Wrote Abu Kamal: "My restless aspiration is to
murder as many of them as possible, and I have decided to
strike at their own den in New York, and at the very Empire
State Building in particular."[4]

More recently, on July 4, 2002, an Egyptian immigrant,
Hesham Mohamed Hadayet, opened fire with two pistols at an
El Al ticket counter at Tom Bradley International Airport in

Los Angeles, killing two. Once again, U.S. authorities were at pains to stress that the gunman was mentally unbalanced and a "lone wolf," but once again, ample evidence showed that his actions were rational in broader terms. In 1992, Hadayet had sought political asylum in the United States but was turned down by the Immigration and Naturalization Service, which suggested he was concealing his membership in a violent fundamentalist organization aimed at overthrowing the Egyptian government and establishing an Islamic state. FBI and police investigations also disclosed his passionate hatred of Israel and the fact that he had plotted the attack on the El Al ticket counter for weeks.

Apart from these major episodes, the Anti-Defamation League reports an upsurge since the mid-1990s of more "spontaneous" violence connected to the Middle East and in most cases perpetrated by Arabs. This became especially pronounced after the eruption in Israel of Yasir Arafat's second intifada in September 2000. Within months, at least thirty-four incidents—primarily vandalism and arson but not excluding physical attacks on individuals—were reported in New York State alone. Thanks in part to heightened security after September 11, violence of this kind has declined, but there have been disturbing outbreaks—including in Berkeley, California, where "Jewish residents have been attacked on the streets," as the *Daily Californian* reported in April 2002, and the city's mayor was driven to propose a special police unit to deal with a rash of death threats against Jews and bomb scares at local synagogues.[5] Accurate statistics about this kind of low-level violence and harassment are not available, but such activities do not develop in a vacuum. As in Europe, incitement of hatred against Jews is a significant factor in certain quadrants of Muslim America.

❖

One major source of agitation, again as in Europe, is the proliferating number of Islamic "educational" institutions at the elementary and secondary level, some of them sponsored or

105

subsidized by Arab countries, especially Saudi Arabia. The oil-rich kingdom has long been engaged in what the *New York Times* calls a "costly and quietly insistent campaign to spread its state religion" in the United States.[6] Toward that end, it has been spending millions to fund the construction of mosques and schools. It has also been bringing Americans to Saudi Arabia for religious training. These Americans, immersed in the fine points of Wahhabi Islam with its extreme anti-Semitic teachings, are then expected to return to the United States and find positions as imams in mosques or instructors in Islamic schools. Although the exact number of such schools is unknown, the *Washington Post* has offered a range of between 200 and 600, with no fewer than 30,000 students enrolled in any given year. In addition to day schools, there are weekend schools attended by thousands more.[7]

What is taught in these institutions? From the little reporting that has been done by the *Washington Post,* the *New York Times,* the *Daily News* and others, a disturbing picture emerges. At the Islamic Saudi Academy, a school in Northern Virginia, for example, one finds the normal American high school curriculum of pre-calculus, American history, physics and so on, plus religious and political instruction. Under the latter rubrics, students are taught that the Day of Judgment promised in the Qur'an cannot arrive until, among other things, "Muslims start attacking Jews." At the al-Qalam All-Girls School in Springfield, Virginia, visiting reporters observed seventh-grade students discussing in class whether Osama bin Laden is a victim of prejudice, while on the walls hung maps of the Middle East without any state of Israel. Textbooks published in Pakistan were in use, though one teacher apologetically explained that she never used the pages "portraying Jews as treacherous people who financially 'oppress' others."[8]

No such scruples seem to inhibit Islamic schools that have sprung up in and around New York City. Two reporters for the *Daily News* spent three months examining textbooks used in institutions like the Ideal Islamic School in Long Island City, the Muslim Center Elementary School in Flushing,

Queens, and the al-Noor School in Brooklyn. At the Ideal Islamic School, fifth and sixth graders were being taught that "the Jews [had] killed their own prophets and disobeyed Allah."[9] At the Muslim Center Elementary School, sixth, seventh and eighth graders were using a textbook, *What Islam Is All About,* according to which Jews "subscribe to a belief in racial superiority.... Their religion even teaches them to call down curses upon the worship places of non-Jews whenever they pass by them! They arrogantly refer to anyone who is not Jewish as 'gentiles,' equating them with sin." The same text goes on to explain that the "reasons for Jewish hostility lie in their general characteristics" and that "You will ever find [Jews] deceitful, except for a few of them." More than forty thousand copies of *What Islam Is All About* are said to be in use in Islamic schools in the United States. Its author, Abidullah al-Ansari Ghazi, told the *Daily News* that he wrote the anti-Semitic passages some "ten, twenty years ago. And, to tell you the truth, I based it on the classical sources, which are much harsher than what I wrote here."[10]

Schools are not the only means by which such hatred is disseminated in the United States, and impressionable youngsters are not the only audience. A dense network of social and political institutions is similarly preoccupied. In his study of Islamist extremism, *American Jihad,* Steven Emerson describes the activities of the Islamic Association for Palestine, an organization established in Chicago in 1981 that has served as the U.S. arm of Hamas. Its annual conferences have featured incendiary speeches against the Jews: in 1989, an Egyptian "religious scholar" told his Kansas City audience that "Palestine cannot be liberated except by Islam!.... On the Hour of Judgment, the Muslims will fight the Jews and kill them, until the Jews will hide behind the stone, and the stone and the tree will say, O Servant of Allah, O Muslim! There is a Jew behind me, come and kill him." Another speech at the same gathering, by a Kuwait-based Palestinian cleric, offered "greetings to those who shoot at the Jews with the catapult, and to those who poke out the eyes of the Jews with the slingshot."[11]

Arab-language newspapers published in this country carry more of the same. In Paterson, New Jersey, where a sizable Arab population has settled, the *Arab Voice,* the main local weekly, has reprinted excerpts from the *Protocols of the Elders of Zion.* (Of course, the editor of the paper offered a disclaimer, to the effect that "no one can prove if the *Protocols* are true or if they are not," adding in an interview that "You give the people the idea and they decide.")[12] In mosques and Islamic bookstores across the United States, inflammatory pamphlets and cassettes are on sale, all to the same end.

In early 2003, Michelle Goldberg, a reporter for *Salon,* interviewed worshippers at the al-Farooq mosque in Brooklyn. This is not, to be sure, a typical house of worship. It was here, according to Attorney General John Ashcroft, that al-Qaeda raised some $20 million, and here that Sheikh Omar Abdel Rahman, the one-eyed cleric now serving a life sentence for his role in the first World Trade Center bombing, acted as imam in the early 1990s, preaching a fanatical brand of anti-Semitic and anti-American hatred. What the blind sheikh taught a decade ago has not been forgotten. One Algerian émigré told Goldberg that "accusations against the mosque are 'Jewish propaganda, from the Jewish media.'" Another worshipper, from Tunisia, had a similar reaction: "It's a lie fabricated by Jews."[13]

While Egyptian émigré extremists have held sway at some mosques, Saudi-trained extremists have gained influence in others. According to Faheem Shuaibe, an imam at a major black mosque in Oakland, California, and a frequent traveler to Saudi Arabia, there has been "a very deliberate recruitment process by the Saudis, trying to find black Muslims who had a real potential for Islamic learning and also for submission to their agenda."[14] The presence of such extremists in mosques across the country has been a major concern of U.S. law enforcement authorities in the wake of September 11. The Justice Department has been weighing a directive instructing FBI field offices to tally the number of local mosques in their jurisdictions for the purpose of counterterrorism investigations; in some locations, FBI agents have requested membership rolls directly from mosques and from Islamic organizations. Not surprisingly, both policies remain under dispute.

❖

If immigration from Arab countries and the larger Muslim world serves as one conduit of Islamic extremism and anti-Semitism, there are indigenous channels as well; in some cases, the two varieties have begun to cross-fertilize. The best-known instance is the Reverend Louis Farrakhan and his organization, the Nation of Islam. Farrakhan himself has a long history of openly anti-Semitic utterances: he has described Adolf Hitler as "a very great man [who] rose Germany up from the ashes of defeat"; he has said that "the small numbers of Jewish people in the United States...exercise a tremendous amount of influence on the affairs of government...they exercise extraordinary control, and black people will never be free in this country until they are free of that kind of control"; he has said that the state of Israel will never be able to live in peace with its neighbors because "there can be no peace structured on injustice, thievery, lying and deceit and using the name of God to shield your dirty religion."[15] Farrakhan's right-hand man for many years, Khalid Abdul Muhammed, went further, descending into the pornographic imagery that one might find in the Nazi publication *Der Stürmer.* The Nation of Islam regularly publishes viciously anti-Semitic remarks in its newspaper, the *Final Call,* and its bookstores carry classics of anti-Semitic propaganda, including the *Protocols of the Elders of Zion.* Tracts of its own devising include a pseudoscholarly tome, bulging with footnotes, entitled *The Secret Relationship between Blacks and Jews,* with chapter headings like "Jews and the Rape of Black Women."

Given his anti-Semitic orientation, it hardly comes as a surprise that as far back as 1984, Farrakhan was already seeking financial and other assistance from the Arab world, traveling to Libya to meet with its leader, Colonel Muammar al-Qaddafi. In 1985, Farrakhan boasted of a $5 million loan from the Libyan strongman, describing him as "a fellow struggler in the cause of liberation of our people."[16] In 1996, he embarked upon a multination tour of the Middle East, announcing on his return that he had received a $1 billion pledge from the Libyan government and established a promising relationship with Saddam Hussein. In 2002, Farrakhan again visited Baghdad, where he was quoted declaring that "the Muslim American people are praying to the almighty God to grant victory to Iraq."[17]

Although he has made no secret either of his anti-Semitic ideas or of his ties to enemies of the United States, he has nevertheless been admitted to some polite company. Wallace Deen Muhammad, the imam who leads the main organizational body of American black Muslims, the Muslim American Society, declared in February 2000 that he wished to convey a "message of peace and love and undying friendship to Louis Farrakhan."[18] Nor has Farrakhan's message been a barrier to acceptance among some non-Muslim blacks. Opinion polls have long shown that black Americans register the highest levels of anti-Semitic attitudes of any subgroup in the United States—a complicated subject that we need not explore here—and a number of black political leaders appear not only unperturbed by Farrakhan's anti-Semitism but prepared to make common cause with him on a range of issues. In 1993, as head of the NAACP, former congressman Kweise Mfume gave Farrakhan a ticket to respectability by entering his own organization into a "sacred covenant" with the Nation of Islam. At Farrakhan's now-famous Million Man March in October 1995, sharing the stage were not only well-known fellow extremists and anti-Semites but also icons of the civil rights movement like Rosa Parks, the poet Maya Angelou and the Reverend Jesse Jackson. More recently, Farrakhan has been embraced by the black intellectual Cornel West.

Louis Farrakhan is by no means the whole story of Islam in black America. American prisons, where the numbers of black men have increased in the past two decades to almost 800,000, have proved an exceptionally fertile ground for Muslim proselytizing; it is estimated that today there are approximately 200,000 to 340,000 Muslim inmates, constituting some 10 to 17 percent of the total prison population. Servicing the religious needs of this population has required hiring Muslim chaplains: New York State, with the fourth-largest prison system in the nation, employs 45; California employs 18; the Federal Bureau of Prisons employs 10.

Islamic institutions undertake "outreach" programs among inmates in prisons across the country. Some of this activity is entirely innocuous, entailing the distribution of copies of the Qur'an and other religious texts. Some of it is anything but innocuous. Much is underwritten by the government of Saudi Arabia, whose embassy in Washington supplies religious pamphlets and videos to prison chaplains across the United States and also regularly invites chaplains to Saudi Arabia for religious training. One beneficiary of this largesse is Wallace Gene Marks, whose story was told by the journalist Paul Barrett in the *Wall Street Journal.*

Marks is a former black radical who in 1971 was part of the Harlem Five, a group of would-be terrorists tried on conspiracy-to-murder charges. Marks himself was convicted of possessing illegal firearms. In prison, he became affiliated with Farrakhan's Nation of Islam and changed his name to Wallace 10X. After serving his term, Marks was hired by New York State to be one of the first Muslim chaplains in its prison system. At some point after that, he left Farrakhan to join a more orthodox Sunni group and changed his name to Warith Deen Umar. He then began to receive religious training in Saudi Arabia, and in subsequent years was invited there repeatedly. Umar also earned a master's degree at the Graduate School of Islamic and Social Sciences in Leesburg, Virginia, some of whose students received scholarship funds from the governments of Malaysia and Kuwait; the school was raided by U.S. officials after September 11 as part of an investigation into the funneling of Saudi money to terrorist groups including Hamas and al-Qaeda.

Warith Deen Umar ministered to thousands of prisoners

111

over a period of two decades. He also was eventually given responsibility for recruiting and training Muslim chaplains across the state and became a consultant to the U.S. Bureau of Prisons. But even as he performed these duties, Umar was simultaneously promoting another agenda: advancing an extremist version of Islam that included support for the hijackers of September 11. "Even Muslims who say they are against terrorism secretly admire and applaud" the September 11 hijackers, he wrote in a document obtained by the *Wall Street Journal;* and prison, he added, "is the perfect recruitment and training grounds for radicalism and the Islamic religion."[19] There is abundant evidence that Umar is right. José Padilla, the U.S. citizen detained as an "enemy combatant" for helping to plot an attack on a major American city with a radiological "dirty bomb," converted to Islam after a prison spell in Florida, changed his name to Abdullah al-Mujahir, and eventually traveled to Afghanistan or Pakistan to wage jihad with al-Qaeda.

Padilla's case may be exceptional, but Umar's is not; New York's commissioner of prisons acknowledged to the *Journal* that "a large group" of prison chaplains had "traveled at the Saudi government's expense."[20] And the Wahhabi extremism in which these chaplains are immersed seems to be finding a receptive audience, according to the *Journal* report. It's true that the Jewish question per se does not appear to be a major preoccupation of these chaplains. But neither is it entirely absent—forming, as it does, an integral part of the doctrine absorbed through the Saudi-funded education they receive in the tenets and worldview of their faith.

❖

If the pathogen of Arab and Islamic anti-Semitism has made its way to the United States, it has found here a host body less receptive to its powers than in Europe. Less receptive—but not wholly unreceptive.

As we have already noted, the far Right has been a traditional breeding ground for anti-Semitism in this country, but it is one steadily shrinking in size and influence. The World Church of the Creator, the Aryan Nations, the National Alliance, the Liberty Lobby, the splinter factions of the Ku Klux Klan—occasionally these groups perpetrate violent crimes, but none of them is in the least impressive. Nor is their decline difficult to explain. In the aftermath of Timothy McVeigh's bombing of the federal building in Oklahoma City in 1995, extremist groups on the Right not only have been subjected to ever closer scrutiny but also have fallen to unprecedented levels of public disrepute.

The founder of the stridently anti-Semitic World Church of the Creator, Ben Klassen, killed himself in 1993; his successor, Matt Hale, known for using an Israeli flag as a doormat on which to wipe his boots, is in federal custody on charges of plotting to murder a judge. The Aryan Nations, for its part, is not exactly a mass movement; in the year 2001, it was believed to have a grand total of one hundred members. The National Alliance, a neo-Nazi organization, is reported by the ADL to be "a top cause for concern," but its last leader, William Pierce, died in his trailer home in 2002 at the age of sixty-nine.[21]

Among the more successful of fringe anti-Semites is David Duke, a former Ku Klux Klan leader who has expressed support for Nazis. In 1987, Duke was elected to the Louisiana House of Representatives. In 1990, his candidacy for a seat in the U.S. Senate drew nearly 40 percent of the vote, forcing a runoff election. Duke next ran for governor of Louisiana in 1991, once again forcing a runoff and once again losing. This marked the apogee of his political career. His 1992 campaign for the U.S. presidency never got off the ground. Today, Duke is not exactly poised to start afresh: in April 2003, he reported to a federal prison in Texas to serve a fifteen-month sentence for mail and tax fraud, having bilked his followers out of hundreds of thousands of dollars in a fundraising swindle.

Closer to the mainstream is Patrick J. Buchanan, who over the years has embraced a number of anti-Semitic causes and ideas. Buchanan has chosen to defend war criminals like John Demjanjuk, who served as a guard at a Nazi death camp; he has praised Adolf Hitler as "an individual of great courage, a soldier's soldier in the Great War,...[a] genius"; and he has flirted with Holocaust denial, asserting that diesel engines of the kind used by the Nazis to exterminate Jews "did not emit enough carbon monoxide to kill anybody."[22] Although Buchanan is an attractive television personality, a highly skilled debater and a seasoned author of best-selling books, his aspirations for political office have been a bust. His run for the presidency in 2000 on the Reform Party ticket drew less than 1 percent of the vote—a major embarrassment for someone claiming to be a "populist." In the wake of his defeat, Buchanan joined with the Greek journalist Taki Theodoracopulos, another writer with well-established anti-Semitic credentials, to publish a magazine, the *American Conservative,* which in its first year fervently opposed U.S. intervention in Iraq on the grounds that it would only serve the interests of Israel. So far, his publication seems to have acquired little of a readership.

It is not, in any case, his enemies on the Left—or "the Jews"—that are the problem for Buchanan, but his putatively fellow conservatives. The fact is that extremist and anti-Semitic ideas find little traction on the contemporary Right. Jude Wanniski, for example, formerly a distinguished member of the *Wall Street Journal* editorial board and the author of *The Way the World Works,* a popular book on supply-side economics, became virtually a pariah among conservatives when he chose to become a defender of Louis Farrakhan and to denounce "the Jewish establishment" for having "bought both political parties with campaign funds and with its Enforcer, the Anti-Defamation League."[23] Similarly, Joseph Sobran, once a regular and well-regarded columnist for the conservative *National Review,* found himself thrust aside after he wrote a series of blatantly anti-Semitic articles.*

---

*A similar fate may be enveloping the actor-producer Mel Gibson, who adheres to an ultra-traditionalist branch of Catholicism and whose film *The Passion,* about the crucifixion of Jesus Christ, was provoking fierce controversy even before it assumed final form.

❖

The contrast with the situation on the Left could not be more stark, both at the elite level and at the grassroots. Here the primary focus is less on the supposed misdeeds of the Jews than on the supposed perfidy of the "Jew of the nations," the state of Israel—denounced in terms so lurid and extravagant as to betray an underlying anti-Semitic sentiment.

Some elements are already an old story. "[H]ow dangerous...is the anti-Semitic ideology being developed by the growing black movement?" was the question posed by the sociologist Earl Raab in the pages of *Commentary* as early as 1969. The Black Power movement, Raab went on, "has already succeeded in reintroducing political anti-Semitism as a fashionable item in the American public arena—with what consequences no one can yet tell."[24]

Some three decades later, those consequences may not appear terribly alarming. There have been major Jewish-vs.-black collisions—the black riot against the Jews of Crown Heights, Brooklyn, in 1991 being the most significant example. The famed "black-Jewish coalition" that was so long a staple of American political activism—and mythology—is now a thing of the distant past. But the cooling of mutual expectations has not been altogether bad. The Black Panthers and the militants who slurred Jewish teachers in the Ocean Hill–Brownsville dispute have long since passed from the scene, and the intense anxieties that black anti-Semitism provoked in the Jewish community in those years have abated. In the intervening decades, prominent black politicians who have strayed into the *open* expression of anti-Semitism—recall the Reverend Jesse Jackson's description of New York as "Hymietown" in 1984—have been induced to issue apologies (though without losing their honored place in liberal society).

That at least is the impression. It is not false; nonetheless, it is misleading. For if Jewish anxieties about black anti-Semitism are today less acute, this is only partly traceable to a reduction in friction between the two groups. A significant

115

quotient of anti-Semitism continues to exist in the black community, manifested in the eagerness of American black leaders in Congress and elsewhere to denounce Israel and take the side of its murderous adversaries. The plain fact is that this has become the norm. It has lost its shock value, and it is now expected and even accepted, not only by the Jewish community but by the political culture at large.

One such leader is Cynthia McKinney, who throughout her tenure as a congresswoman from Georgia made a point of sticking it to the Jews. In addition to her consistent support for the radical Palestinian cause, in 1994 McKinney adamantly refused to condemn a speech by Khalid Muhammed of the Nation of Islam in which he accused the "so-called Jews" of "sucking our blood in the black community."[25] After September 11, in perfect harmony with propaganda emanating from the Arab world, she suggested that President Bush may have had advance knowledge of the terrorist attack and had even personally profited from it. McKinney's campaign for Congress in 2002 enjoyed the fervent support of Louis Farrakhan, who repeatedly blamed the Jewish lobby for her faltering standing in the polls. When she eventually lost her primary battle to another black candidate, her father explained that the election had hinged on one word alone, which he spelled out: "J-E-W-S."[26] None of McKinney's behavior deterred more mainstream politicians, including Democratic House whip Nancy Pelosi and sixteen members of the Congressional Black Caucus, from backing her to the hilt.

A similar story can be told about a 2002 congressional race in Alabama involving the black incumbent Earl Hilliard. In the course of his campaign against his challenger Artur Davis, a black federal prosecutor, Hilliard's staff distributed a flier entitled, "Davis and the Jews, No Good for the Black Belt." It urged voters to reject Davis because, among other things, he supported Israel's "policy of complete domination." It was Israel, the pamphlet continued, that "stood with apartheid in South Africa," so asking blacks to vote for Davis would be "like asking a chicken to vote for Colonel Sanders—

they can expect nothing short of misery and death."[27] Though Hilliard, like McKinney, was defeated in the primary contest, some two dozen of his fellow Democratic congressmen, many of them members of the Congressional Black Caucus, contributed funds to his campaign, and so did the Democratic Congressional Campaign Committee, one of the party's main funding arms.

Perhaps the most vivid example of the same "outrage gap," as it might be termed, concerns the Reverend Al Sharpton. Back in 1988, this street activist was a central figure in the Tawana Brawley hoax, serving as an "adviser" to a sixteen-year-old black girl who had leveled spurious kidnapping and abuse charges against six white men. Sharpton accused New York State's Jewish attorney general, Robert Abrams, of behaving like a "Nazi" in his conduct of the investigation. In 1991, in the immediate aftermath of the Crown Heights riot where a mob chanted "kill the Jews" and placards screamed "Hitler didn't do his job"—the riot culminated in the stabbing death of a Hasidic Jew named Yankel Rosenbaum—Sharpton openly fanned the embers of anti-Semitism in a speech declaiming against "Oppenheimer in South Africa [who] sends diamonds straight to Tel Aviv and deals with the diamond merchants here in Crown Heights."[28] In 1995, Sharpton targeted Freddy's, a Jewish-owned store in Harlem, with a boycott and a picket line; over the course of weeks, anti-Semitic signs and chants were regularly seen and heard, and at one point a Sharpton follower entered the store and reportedly shouted, "I will be back to burn the Jew store down." In due course, he did just that, killing eight employees.[29]

But in the fall of 2003, a man who only yesterday was a street thug with anti-Semitic proclivities, who proudly associated with Louis Farrakhan and had never issued a word of regret for the harm he wrought, became a candidate for the U.S. presidency, treated by the Democratic Party as a member in good standing and by the media as a respectable politician. On stage, in nationally televised debates with his fellow candidates, Sharpton was never subjected to a word of reproach or

117

even a hint of criticism. Daniel Patrick Moynihan's classic phrase, "defining deviancy down," cannot have had a more clear-cut embodiment.

❖

In American politics, anti-Semitism is taboo—except, as we have seen, when it is expressed by groups or individuals operating under special moral exemptions. This tells us that we are dealing less with a political issue in the normal sense than with a cultural issue. And it is indeed to the arena of culture and education that we must turn, for it is there that we can best trace the inroads of anti-Semitism into the lives of Americans today.

In the 1960s, the poet Amiri Baraka, then known as LeRoi Jones, was a radical activist associated with the Black Panthers. In 2002, he was appointed by the governor of New Jersey as the state's poet laureate. Shortly after this title was bestowed upon him, Baraka appeared at a festival and recited a poem, "Somebody Blew Up America," in which he suggested that Israel had advance knowledge of the September 11 attacks:

> Who knew the World Trade Center was gonna get bombed
> Who told 4,000 Israeli workers at the Twin Towers
> To stay home that day
> Why did Sharon stay away?[30]

Within the Jewish community, this poem immediately created a furor, and in short order, politicians including the governor of New Jersey were calling for the author to step down from his post. But Baraka fought back, proclaiming that his critics were attempting to "repress and stigmatize independent thinkers everywhere."[31] What followed was highly instructive.

Baraka is a known quantity: it is no secret that his work, in the apt description of the black critic Stanley Crouch, represents an "incoherent mix of racism, anti-Semitism, homophobia, black nationalism, anarchy, and ad-hominem attacks."[32] Nevertheless, over the course of his career he has been awarded numerous literary plums, including fellowships from the Guggenheim Foundation and the National Endowment for the Arts. His elevation to the post of poet laureate was not the first time he had been showered with honors for his subpar talents and meretricious ideas.

Now the scandal only continued. From the moment that the governor attempted to remove Baraka from his sinecure, a battalion of liberals and leftists emerged to defend both the poem itself and its author's "rights." To Walter Fields, a former NAACP official, the only thing Baraka did was to "question the behavior of the head of state of Israel."[33] To Wilbert A. Tatum, publisher emeritus of New York's *Amsterdam News,* Baraka's poem was an "epic" and its author one of the great "intellectual leaders of our civilization," having dared in this case "to question who gave word to Jews only that they should escape the World Trade Center before the disaster of 9/11."[34] Unsurprisingly, the *New York Times* editorial page found the poem itself reprehensible, but was careful to hail Baraka as a "powerful and respected poet" and to pronounce "offensive" any attempt "to fire or silence him."[35]

Thrust into the limelight of controversy, Baraka was soon on the lecture circuit. He was invited to recite his poem at Stanford University within two days of a speech by Israel's former prime minister Ehud Barak, leading the *Stanford Daily* to congratulate the university for promoting "freedom of expression through open dialogue."[36] At Wellesley, two separate departments—art and Africana studies—teamed up with three student organizations to pay Baraka several thousand dollars to recite his anti-Semitic verses. At Yale, Baraka's recitation met with a standing ovation.

Baraka has not been the only poet to win acclaim on campuses as an anti-Semite. The Oxford poet Tom Paulin, whom we met earlier, was invited to become a lecturer at Columbia University not long after his verses about the "Zionist SS" appeared. As with Baraka, controversy descended, and so did invitations to give readings across the land, including at the

University of Vermont, Princeton and Harvard. Paulin was asked to give the Harvard English department's distinguished Morris Gray Lecture in Poetry; when a campus-wide protest ensued, he was disinvited but then reinvited.

Then there was the acclaimed feminist poet Marilyn Hacker of New York's City College. Fond of equating Jews with Nazis, she wrote that

> Jews who learned their comportment from storm-troopers
> act out the nightmares that woke their grandmothers
> Jews sit, black-clad, claim peace.[37]

It was easy to find more of the same sort of thing in web anthologies of poems written against the war in Iraq. "They hate war, but not a war against the Jews," wrote a perceptive commentator in *Jewish Week.*[38]

❖

Poets deal in words—in heightened speech. Others use words explicitly to incite, or go straight to action. At institutions of higher learning across the country, the list of outrageous incidents has gotten long and is still growing. At Indiana University, someone left a bust of Hitler on Holocaust Remembrance Day with a note saying, "Thanks to the man who made it all possible."[39] At the University of Colorado at Boulder, the campus Hillel Society received threatening phone calls and a rock was hurled through one of its windows. At Rutgers University, the organizer of something called the National Student Conference of the Palestine Solidarity Movement announced that Israel "is an apartheid, colonial settler state," and that "I do not believe apartheid, colonial settler states have a right to exist."[40] In a student newspaper, the *Medium,* appeared the words: "Die Jew. Die, die, die, die, die, die. Stop living, die, die, DIE! Do us all a favor and build yourself [an]...oven."[41] At the University of California, San Diego, the student association funded a campus-wide "Anti-Zionism Week." There, according to one student who attended, an abundance of anti-Semitic material was distributed, including selections from the

Protocols of the Elders of Zion and falsified quotations from the Talmud in which it was made to appear that Jewish males have license to rape gentile females over the age of three. Pro-Palestinian demonstrators placed mock corpses of infants along a path and chanted, "Jews have killed our babies."[42]

From the lips of a tenured professor at Georgetown: "How have Judaism, the Jews, and the international forces all permitted Zionism to become a wild, destructive beast capable of perpetrating atrocities?"[43] At the University of Chicago, a university-appointed preceptor told a Jewish student he would not read her BA paper because it focused on topics relating to Judaism and Zionism. On the same campus, an "Anti-Zionist Manifesto" was distributed containing photos of bleeding Palestinian children and equating the Jewish star with the swastika.[44]

In the San Francisco Bay Area, a center of left-wing radicalism, anti-Semitic activity has been particularly intense. At the University of California at Berkeley, graffiti reading "Fuck the Jews" were emblazoned on the Hillel building and a cinder block was hurled through its front door.[45] Students reciting the mourner's prayer during a vigil for Holocaust Remembrance Day were shouted down by protesters honoring the memory of suicide bombers. Official approval was granted to an undergraduate English course entitled "Politics and Poetics of Palestinian Resistance," which included as its subject matter the "right of Palestinians to fight for their own self-determination" and against "the brutal Israeli occupation of Palestine."[46]

At nearby San Francisco State University, whose declared mission is to foster "respect for and appreciation of scholarship, freedom, human diversity, and the cultural mosaic of the City of San Francisco," matters have been far worse. Over the past decade and a half, according to Laurie Zoloth, the chair of the Jewish studies department, the university has accumulated a track record as "a place that teaches anti-Semitism, hatred for America, and hatred, above all else, for the Jewish state of Israel."[47] On one occasion, Jewish students identifying themselves as members of a Zionist campus group were spat upon and greeted with shouts of *"Sieg Heil"* at an antiwar demonstration. A professor of international relations explained in his lectures that major bureaucracies of the U.S. government, including the Department of Defense and the Treasury, are "beholden to Jewish interests," that Jewish bankers "have bought the Congress," and that the U.S. president "has to toe the Jewish line."[48] The Pan Afrikan Student Union erected a mural, commissioned and paid for by the student council, depicting Jewish stars covered in dollar bills.

All this activity came to a culmination in the spring of 2002, when the campus of San Francisco State was blanketed with slogans like "Zionism equals racism" and "Jews equals Nazis," and with posters showing cans labeled "canned Palestinian children meat, slaughtered according to Jewish rites under American license." On May 7, when some fifty Jewish undergraduates affiliated with Hillel organized a rally for Middle East peace, they were surrounded by a threatening mob chanting slogans like "Hitler did not finish the job," "Fuck the Jews," "Die, racist pigs" and "Go back to Russia."[49]

If, in Europe, left-wing academics have been campaigning to sever ties between their institutions and Israeli researchers, left-wing professors in America's major universities have been promoting a "Divest from Israel" campaign, gathering signatures on a petition demanding that their institutions sell off investments in companies that do business in Israel. Hundreds of professors from colleges and universities have signed this document, which claims an "appalling" record of "human-rights abuses against Palestinians at the hands of the Israeli government."[50]

Is the petition drive anti-Semitic? The answer seems fairly clear. Israel is a democracy operating under the rule of law with a well-functioning judicial system and a free press. If it has engaged in abuses of human rights during the course of its decades-long effort to secure its survival against war and terrorism, these abuses have typically been exposed by Israelis themselves. There are, also, dozens upon dozens of countries around the world whose human rights records are worse than Israel's by several orders of magnitude. Among them are grotesque and systematic violators—Saudi Arabia and the People's Republic of China, to name two—that host major corporations whose stocks are held in the investment portfolios of American universities. To criticize Israel for its policies is a perfectly legitimate enterprise. To target the Jewish state as if it were somehow the most flagrant human rights transgressor in the world, the single country in need of sanctions, is nothing more than unadorned bigotry.

Precisely this consideration finally prompted the president of Harvard, Lawrence Summers, to warn in a statement in 2002 that "Serious and thoughtful people [on the Harvard campus] are advocating and taking actions that are anti-Semitic in their effect if not their intent." In California, things got so far out of hand that the state's governor, Gray Davis, felt it necessary to step in; ordering a comprehensive review of all anti-Semitic incidents on the state's campuses, Davis instructed universities to warn incoming students that they would be prosecuted if they committed crimes against Jews or other hate crimes, and to screen course descriptions to ensure that they are "not vehicles for discrimination, intimidation, and hate."[51]

❖

If universities have become prime propagators of anti-Semitism in the United States, the media, deploying their unique powers of amplification, have hardly been derelict. Once again the contours remain the same, as ideas ultimately derived from Arab propaganda, and themselves distant reflections of the notorious *Protocols of the Elders of Zion,* have penetrated the thinking of the Left and thence made their way into the mainstream press. Thus, as the Bush administration began to contemplate taking action against Saddam Hussein, a few antiwar columnists and editorialists suggested that influential Jewish officials were manipulating U.S. foreign policy in the interests of Israel. The charge originated in hints and whispers, a subtle shifting of the spotlight from such high-ranking non-Jewish officials as

Richard Cheney or Donald Rumsfeld or Condoleezza Rice—
or President George Bush—to more subordinate names like
Paul Wolfowitz, the undersecretary of defense and the "spark
plug of the Get Saddam Club" in the words of *New York Times*
columnist Maureen Dowd, or Richard Perle, a "drum-beater"
for war. Other (Jewish) hawks who also repeatedly surfaced in
Dowd's column were the Pentagon official Douglas Feith and
William Kristol of the *Weekly Standard,* stalwarts of "the clique
of conservative intellectuals pushing the war."

As the antiwar movement gathered steam, more direct
versions of the theme circulated widely, and Dowd's winks
about the dark force behind government policy gave way to
the word "Jewish" and other explicit synonyms. In the *Chicago
Tribune,* Fred M. Donner, a professor at the University of
Chicago, complained that the Bush administration's "rosy sce-
nario for the upcoming war against Iraq" was "a vision deriving
from Likud-oriented members of the President's team—particularly Richard Perle, Paul Wolfowitz, and Douglas Feith."
Noting that Perle had once written a memo to Ariel Sharon,
Donner asked: "why is he serving in a high position in an
American administration?"[52] To Stanley Hoffmann of Harvard,
"a loose collection" of individuals who "look[ed] on foreign
policy through the lens of one dominant concern: is it good or
bad for Israel?" were now "well ensconced in the Pentagon,
around such strategists as Paul Wolfowitz, Richard Perle, and
Douglas Feith."[53]

There were many others. Georgie Anne Geyer: "The 'Get
Iraq' campaign...emerged first and particularly from pro-
Israeli hard-liners in the Pentagon such as Deputy Defense
Secretary Paul Wolfowitz and adviser Richard Perle."[54] Joel
Kovel, writing in *Tikkun:* American policy was being formu-
lated by "ardent right-wing Zionists," among whom were
Wolfowitz, Perle, Lewis Libby (chief of staff for Vice Presi-
dent Cheney), Eric Edelman (Libby's former top assistant) and
Elliott Abrams.[55] Paul Buhle, also in *Tikkun:* Perle, Wolfowitz
and Abrams were "conspirators" who linked "global conquest
to Jewish interests," and the appearance of these Jewish

"superhawks" running the U.S. government was "almost as if the anti-Semitic *Protocols of Zion,* successfully fought for a century, [had] suddenly returned with an industrial sized grain of truth."[56] Jason Vest, in the *Nation:* "far-right American Zionists" using "far-right Zionist dollars" and seeing "no difference between U.S. and Israeli national security interests" had sent "dozens of their members...to powerful government posts," there to wage a "relentless campaign for war" with Iraq.[57] Kathleen and Bill Christison, writing in the *Washington Report on Middle East Affairs:* "The issue we are dealing with in the Bush administration is dual loyalties—the double allegiance of those myriad officials at high and middle levels who cannot distinguish U.S. interests from Israeli interests, who baldly promote the supposed identity of interests between the United States and Israel."[58] Edward Said, the Columbia University professor of English, writing in the Egyptian newsweekly *Al-Ahram:* not only were Pentagon officials—"the Perles and Wolfowitzs of this country"—propelling the U.S. into war, but they had an agent in place in the White House in the form of President Bush's spokesman Ari Fleischer, "who I believe is also an Israeli citizen."[59] (This last and false "fact," it was subsequently revealed, seems to have come from neo-Nazi websites.)[60] And on national television, Chris Matthews, the host of *Hardball:* the war with Iraq was being driven by "conservative people out there, some of them Jewish, who...believe we should fight the Arabs and take them down."[61]

The Jewish plot to plunge the country into war received perhaps its most elaborate development from Michael Lind, a former editor at the *National Interest* who in recent years has moved from a quirky conservatism to a quirky leftism. In a pair of articles in the British journal *Prospect,*[62] Lind explained in detail how the Jewish lobby had seized control of American foreign policy. The story is by now familiar: "a cadre of pro-Israel hawks"—the "Wolfowitz-Perle-Feith clique"—had wormed its way into the seats of power and "seized the initiative," so much so that by the summer of 2002, U.S. foreign policy had become "aligned with—if not subordinated to—

that of Ariel Sharon's Israel to a degree that nobody could have imagined." Though the members of this "radical Zionist Right" claimed to speak in the name of American values like democracy, in fact they had one overriding concern: to augment "the power and reputation of Israel."

Where Lind surpassed other conspiracy-mongers was in the elaborateness of his analysis, the shrillness of his tone and the degree of his alarm, real or feigned, for the health and the reputation of the United States. "Thanks to the continuing success of the Israel lobby in manipulating U.S. foreign policy," he wrote, American global leadership was in "far greater danger today" than it had been in recent times.[63] And the danger lay not only abroad: the Jewish lobby had served as a "corrupting influence" on domestic American politics as well. For one thing, it operated as a kind of "ethnic donor machine," funneling money through "phony grassroots" organizations in order to "influence members of Congress in areas where there are few Jewish voters." For another thing, "the disproportionate influence of the Jewish lobby" stifled "uninhibited debate" about America's Middle East policy. In the media, the Jewish lobby had so arranged things that "in the opinion pages and the journals of opinion…propaganda for Israel has free reign." Moreover, the Jews had managed to create an atmosphere of intimidation not unlike the one fomented by Senator Joseph McCarthy in the 1950s: "many journalists and policy experts say in private that they are afraid of being blacklisted by editors and publishers who are zealous Israel supporters."[64]*

❖

With Lind and all the others who harp incessantly on the outsized influence of three or four midlevel Jewish government officials; on Jewish money being funneled through "phony"

---

*Lind's last point was avidly taken up by a left-wing journalist, the *Nation* columnist Eric Alterman, who went so far as to publish a list of American journalists who, presumably on account of dual loyalty, could be "counted upon to support Israel reflexively and without qualification." MSNBC, April 1, 2002.

organizations and "corrupting" our democracy; on the Zionist agenda-pushers; on policymakers who out of dual loyalty have "subordinated" the interests of their country to those of a foreign power; on the policy disaster of global dimensions being brought about by this distortion of the American national interest—with all those who attribute so much sinister power to the "Wolfowitz-Perle-Feith clique," we find a modern replay of a poisonous but well-established tradition.

In 1918, as World War I was reaching its denouement, a publication called the *Anti-Bolshevist* began to appear in New York. One of its major themes, records the historian Léon Poliakov, was that "[t]he Jews were responsible for pushing the United States into the war. They were also maneuvering to make it drag on."[65] The link, according to a series of bogus reports and forgeries that began to appear at the time, was the Bolshevik revolution in Russia: allegedly the work of Jews, primarily American Jews, who had decided to overthrow the czarist government in the interest of assisting Germany, thereby precipitating American entry into the war. In short order, a whole chorus of voices was repeating and embellishing this allegation. According to one contemporaneous American source, the Reverend George A. Simons, a representative of the English Methodist Church in Russia, the 388 members of the Petrograd Soviet were almost all Jews, of whom 265 came from New York. Reverend Simons was duly invited to testify before a U.S. Senate committee:

> *Mr. Simons:* We were told that hundreds of agitators...came from the East Side of New York. I was surprised to find a great number of these men going up and down the Nevski.... We were all struck by the predominance, from the beginning, of the Yiddish element in this affair, and it soon became evident that half the agitators were Jewish.
>
> *Senator Nelson:* Hebrews?
>
> *Mr. Simons:* Hebrews, Jewish apostates. I don't want to speak of Jews as such. I am not in sympathy with anti-Semitism. I never was and never will be. I hate pogroms of any type. But I am firmly convinced that this business is Jewish.[66]

Is the harping on Wolfowitz, Feith and Perle an example of the new anti-Semitism, or the old? The answer, of course, is both. And just as, in the old days, the word "Bolshevik" or "Trotskyite" was used as a thinly veiled synonym for "Jew," so today the term "neoconservative" has insinuated itself into the vocabulary of the antiwar Left as an all-purpose, sinister-sounding substitute for the same word—and with the same lack of precision. For just as not all neoconservatives are Jews, neither do all or most of those formulating administration policy belong to that highly particular movement of ideas known as neoconservatism. Only in the logic of anti-Semitism are these disparate phenomena linked for the purposes of ritualized denunciation and witch-hunting.

Another similarity between the old anti-Semitism and the new, as it happens, is the tacit alliance that has been formed over this question between left-wing intellectuals and commentators and a few radical counterparts on the Right. Among them, Patrick J. Buchanan could be found warning loudly in the pages of his magazine that a "neoconservative clique seeks to ensnare our country in a series of wars that are not in America's interest."[67] These "parasites" and "agents of influence"[68]—Buchanan has cited Wolfowitz, Perle, Feith and Elliott Abrams, among others—"wield disproportionate power" and are, according to Buchanan, fundamentally disloyal to their country.[69]

Much of what Buchanan writes is taken directly from Lind, whom he has quoted abundantly; but these two are not the sole representatives of an emerging "Red-Brown alliance." Both the far Right and the Left favor restrictions on immigration and international trade, and both favor an end to a forward-leaning U.S. foreign policy, also known as a new American "imperialism." But anti-Semitism and hatred of Israel appear to constitute the most powerful adhesive holding together this new coalition—and, improbably enough, the binding agent is the politically active Muslim population in the United States, whose English-language press relentlessly denounces the "Wolfowitz Cabal," i.e., Jewish officials "determined to push the U.S. in the same direction as Israel's most dangerous right-wing policy."[70]

How much damage has the alliance done? Notions swirling around the world of ideas have a way of penetrating the political sphere with astonishing speed. At the populist end, the environmentalists and anarchists who in past years have been satisfied with hurling rocks through the windows of Starbucks coffee shops to protest globalization have now embraced a broader agenda. Joining forces with Palestinian activists and even some skinheads, they are no longer merely chanting, "Hey, hey! Ho, ho! IMF has got to go!" They are now also calumniating the Jewish state under the slogan, "Sharon and Hitler are the same. Only difference is the name."[71]

If one looks upward, at officeholders and aspiring officeholders, one can find echoes of the same or similar themes expressed in more genteel language. Thus we have Gary Hart, a candidate for the U.S. presidency, opining discreetly but pointedly that the terms of U.S. foreign policy must not be "dictated by Americans who too often find it hard to distinguish their loyalties to their original homelands from their loyalties to America and its national interests."[72]

There is also the more revealing case of James Moran, a Democratic congressman who explained to his constituents in northern Virginia that Jewish power was leading our country into a dangerous armed conflict: "If it were not for the strong support of the Jewish community for this war with Iraq, we would not be doing this. The leaders of the Jewish community are influential enough that they could change the direction of where this is going."[73] Moran was roundly chastised for his remarks, not only by Jewish organizations but also by his fellow Democrats, and was rapidly compelled to issue an apology. Why, then, is his case revealing? It illustrates the way in which ideas travel from the pages of small-circulation journals to newspaper op-ed columnists to the speech of politicians seeking the approval of their constituents. And it also illustrates something else: Moran is white. If his offending statement had been uttered by a black Democrat—a Cynthia McKinney or an Earl Hilliard—the response from his fellow Democrats in all likelihood would have been silence. Anti-Semitic ideas are on the loose, but not everyone has been licensed to traffic in them.

❖

This brings us to an especially painful subject—namely, the degree to which such anti-Semitic ideas have been propagated or actually endorsed by some Jews, who thereby legitimate their adoption by others. Indeed, the anti-Semitic Left in the United States (although not, by and large, in Europe) is largely a Jewish contingent.*

The very idea of an anti-Semitic Jew sounds like an oxymoron, but instances of the type go far back in history. What seems to call forth the phenomenon, whether in the Middle Ages or in modern times, is a situation in which the Jewish position in society or in political affairs has been placed under exceptional stress. The "role of renegade Jews, men uprooted and readily thrown off balance, men with 'complexes,' as we would say today," writes Léon Poliakov, "has always been of prime importance during the persecutions of the Jews."[74]

There is a small literature devoted to the subject of "self-hatred," which is the appellation in most common use for those who turn on their own people. Ultimately, the answer must lie in the murky waters of the psychosocial, as individual Jews strive to deflect the poisonous arrows coming at their fellow Jews from larger hostile forces. Throughout history, the personal and psychological advantages conferred by such a disassociation from the Jewish fate were obvious enough.

---

*Among the prominent exceptions is Alexander Cockburn, the prolific columnist for the *Nation* and the founder of a website called Counterpunch, who has likened Israeli military actions to Nazi blitzkriegs and consistently accuses the leaders of the Jewish state of "behaving like war criminals." But Cockburn is an Englishman, an import rather than an indigenous product of the American Left. By the same token, Gore Vidal, who for decades has been pouring vitriol on Israel and bashing American Jews for constituting a subversive "fifth column," is an expatriate, residing most of the time in Italy.

Today, with a worldwide swell of hatred directed against the Jewish state, some Jews are once again striving to turn the arrows away from themselves.

True, in the modern context the vocabulary has changed: Judaism in the current lexicon is pronounced "Zionism." But the intensity of the felt need to vilify the object of hatred has not changed at all. True, in former times men like Theobald of Cambridge, Nicholas Donin or Johannes Pfefferkorn were all self-declared apostates from Judaism, while their counterparts today need undergo no formal conversion to another faith in order to play their role as accusers of Jews. Far from it: as historical irony would have it, trumpeting their Jewish "credentials" even as they denounce the Jewish state and slur its citizens and supporters makes them much more effective exponents of the dishonorable cause they have made their own.

Noam Chomsky, the MIT linguist, is perhaps the best-known case. His intellectual influence is immense. "On an academic list of the ten most frequently cited sources of all time," notes Larissa MacFarquhar in a recent portrait of Chomsky in the *New Yorker,* "he ranks eighth—above Hegel and Cicero, just below Plato and Freud." But when it comes to the Jewish state, this son of a distinguished Hebraist is manifestly a man with—to use Poliakov's term—"a complex." To be completely fair, Israel is not the only object of Chomsky's contumely. MacFarquhar's sketch reveals a scholar who speaks in a quiet and reasonable-sounding monotone until he finds himself in discourse about politics; then he turns "vicious in argument," employing evasions, the crudest forensic tricks and invented facts to make his case.[75]

For years Chomsky has traded in fanatical denunciations of Israel. In his most recent best-selling book, *9-11,* he renders the Jewish homeland as a diabolical entity that strives to inflict the maximum amount of suffering on its Arab neighbors. The Israeli objective, he says in an interview wholly characteristic of his tone and approach, is "large-scale and severe wounding, brutal strangulation of the [Palestinian] population by closures, impassable barriers, and now trenches around cities and villages. Their calculation is that there is a limit to what flesh and blood can endure."[76] Needless to say, he offers no proof or rationale for this insight into Israel's "calculation" in its desperate effort to protect itself from rampant Arab terrorism.

The same image of a country acting with Nazi-like rapacity is favored by Chomsky's acolyte Norman Finkelstein. "[I]f Israelis don't want to stand accused of being Nazis," Finkelstein has explained, "they should simply stop acting like Nazis."[77] Visiting encampments of the terrorist organization Hizbollah in southern Lebanon in 2001 after Israel had withdrawn from its buffer zone there, Finkelstein declared to an audience of Arab students that "I truly honor [Hizbollah fighters] for having inflicted an exceptional and deserving defeat on their foreign occupiers."[78] Finkelstein is himself the child of Holocaust survivors—an autobiographical fact that he continually adduces to bolster his credibility—and is the author of *The Holocaust Industry,* a book arguing that the reparations sought by Jewish victims of Nazism are part of the same "ideological offensive" by which, in pursuit of their "corporate and class interests," American and Israeli Jews oppress American blacks and Palestinian Arabs.[79] Entering the terrain of outright Holocaust denial, Finkelstein even maintains that Jewish organizations have been manufacturing nonexistent Holocaust survivors in the endeavor to fill their coffers and augment their power.

To Joel Kovel, a professor at Bard College, singling out the Jewish state for criticism is by no means a marker of anti-Semitism. In his view, "special criticism of Israel is indeed warranted, in fact, mandatory, simply because Israel is special." Among the attributes that make it special are its ties to the United States, both countries being shining examples of a "messianic settler-colonialism" that aims to oppress the peoples of the Third World. The links between the two countries "have been underwritten and enforced by powerful Zionist lobbies, justified by a press that slavishly follows the party line, rationalized by the liberal intelligentsia, and institutionalized by robotic congressional approval." Most Jews today, whether living in Israel or in the United States, are operating in the service of America's efforts to obtain global domination—"haunted," in Kovel's terms, "by the grotesque metamorphosis of Jewish exceptionalism into a logic of empire."[80]

Chomsky, Finkelstein, Kovel and others do have their counterparts abroad, even in Europe. In August 2002, a group of thirty-eight British intellectuals, including Steven Rose, a professor at the Open University and one of the initiators of the divest-from-Israel petition drive, published an open letter in the *Guardian* renouncing their "unsought" right to live in Israel under the "law of return." Declaring themselves to be "Jews, born and raised outside Israel," they proceeded to indict the Jewish state for its role as an "oppressor" and for its "barbaric" treatment of the Palestinians—a people "forced or terrorized into fleeing" their homeland.[81] The statement said not a single word about the successive wars of aggression that Arab states had waged against Israel since 1948 or the Palestinian acts of terror that were, at that very juncture, taking the lives of Jewish civilians on a daily basis.

But it is in Israel itself that dissent from government policy more often crosses the line into Jewish anti-Semitism. To Uri Avnery, a radical journalist who writes for a variety of publications including the *Arab-American News,* Israel's wonted image as a refuge for Jews fleeing oppression has been replaced by a more accurate picture: "a cruel, brutal, and colonizing state, oppressing a small and helpless people. The persecuted has become the persecutor, David has turned into Goliath." In the United States, Avnery asserts, the ubiquitous and omnipotent "Jewish lobby" every few years "'eliminates' an American politician who does not support the Israeli government unconditionally." Avnery names former congresswoman Cynthia McKinney as the most recent victim of the "Jewish establishment" in its determination to show that "criticizing Sharon is tantamount to political suicide."[82]

In the same Israel-bashing league is the Israeli "new" historian Ilan Pappe, one of a dozen or so Israeli academics to have signed the European petition calling for a boycott of

Israeli academics— i.e., a boycott of themselves. Pappe has made a career of debunking what he calls Israel's founding "myths," in the meantime creating his own myths of an Israel founded in sin, including the sin of mass murder of Palestinian Arabs. And then there is the slightly different figure of Israel Shahak (who died in 2001), a professor of chemistry at the Hebrew University in Jerusalem, a survivor of the Nazis' Bergen-Belsen concentration camp and a slanderer of Israel as a "terrorist state." Shahak devoted much of his life to applying to the contemporary era the "theological" teachings of the classic early-eighteenth-century anti-Semitic text *Entdecktes Judentum* ("Judaism Unmasked") by Johann Andreas Eisenmenger, in which the Talmud appears as a kind of sorcerer's recipe book commanding the Jews to do evil unto the gentiles. "Judaism, especially in its classical form," wrote Shahak in his 1994 tract, *Jewish History, Jewish Religion: The Weight of Three Thousand Years* (with a preface by Gore Vidal), "is totalitarian in nature."[83]

❖

Figures like Chomsky, Finkelstein, Avnery *et al.* fall on the far end of a continuum. In much of what he writes, Finkelstein echoes the revisionist historians who claim that Holocaust reparations are a "racket" used by avaricious Jews to enrich themselves. Chomsky, for his part, has been in open alliance with Holocaust deniers, having written a fawning preface to a book by Robert Faurisson, a professor of French literature who contends that the Holocaust never happened, that the Nazis didn't use gas chambers to exterminate European Jews, and that Anne Frank's diary is a fraud. "I see no anti-Semitic implication in the denial of the existence of gas chambers or even in the denial of the Holocaust," Chomsky has written.[84]

Until recently, none of these figures made much headway outside far-Left circles. Lately, however, they are expanding their appeal. Shahak's writings have become a basic staple of the anti-Semitic library, are widely available in English, French, German and Arabic, and have been posted on the Internet by anti-Semitic groups of both the fringe Right and the radical Left. Avnery's writings are available on Counterpunch, the website of the radical journalist Alexander Cockburn, whose work has in turn been subsidized by the Institute of Arab Studies, a front group for the radical Arab Left. Norman Finkelstein's book on the "Holocaust Industry" was a bestseller in Germany, where its author became a household name as he explained the "fraud" being perpetrated against German taxpayers by wealthy American Jews in the name of Zionism.

Though Chomsky's political influence has been confined largely to university campuses, abroad he is a superstar with a huge following among the wider public. "Wherever he goes," writes Larissa MacFarquhar, "he is sought after by mainstream politicians and the mainstream press, and when he speaks it is to audiences of thousands, sometimes tens of thousands."[85] Even here in the United States, where the linguist does not exercise quite such magnetic attraction, his radical anti-Israeli stance finds an echo, particularly in the larger world of Jewish Left-liberals. The principal activity of a new organization called Jews for Peace in Palestine and Israel is organizing rallies in support of the PLO; and a host of other Jewish groups mimicking Arab propaganda have sprouted up, including, in New York, Jews Against the Occupation, and in the San Francisco Bay Area, A Jewish Voice for Peace. Not the brainchildren of Noam Chomsky in any literal sense, these are nonetheless among his spiritual progeny.

So, for that matter, is the International Solidarity Movement (ISM), an organization of self-proclaimed "international activists" working to promote the Palestinian cause by "nonviolent" methods but also recognizing the Palestinian right to conduct "legitimate armed struggle," i.e., shootings and suicide bombings of Israeli civilians. The ISM was cofounded by Adam Shapiro, a Jew from Brooklyn who in 2002 succeeded in entering Yasir Arafat's compound in Ramallah while it was encircled by Israeli tanks. Since then, Shapiro has specialized in making lurid Chomsky-like accusations against the Jewish state: Israel's forces have been carrying out "summary executions" in Palestinian "camps," he claims, while "raping the [Palestinian] cities and...going in and carrying out terrorist action, going house to house, much like the Nazis did in World War II."[86] Shapiro has also toured the Muslim countries of Asia as a guest of the "Deir Yassin Remembered" Committee, an organization devoted to commemorating an Israeli "massacre" of Arab civilians in 1948.[87] At the very moment that Malaysia's prime minister, Mahathir Mohamad, was distributing copies of Henry Ford's classic, *The International Jew,* to tens of thousands of delegates attending his party's annual conference,[88] Shapiro was in Malaysia telling an audience of local journalists that the Western press "has been grossly unfair in its reporting on the Israeli-Palestinian conflict," ignoring the "injustice and atrocities committed by the Israeli army."[89]

❖

We have not quite finished with the gruesome tale of Jewish anti-Semitism. If there is a hardcore anti-Zionist element in it, there is also something that might be characterized, still more improbably, as a hardcore pro-Zionist element. This particular cadre professes to believe in the idea of an independent Jewish state, but is so profoundly disappointed with the actually existing one as to depict it in terms every bit as bilious as those employed by a Noam Chomsky. It is willing to form alliances with out-and-out adversaries of the Jewish people, and (even while holding aloft the flag of pacifism) to justify violence against Israel and the Jews living there.

Rabbi Michael Lerner, editor of *Tikkun* magazine, is perhaps the most familiar exemplar of this disposition. At the height of the second Palestinian intifada, Lerner and hundreds of his associates in the "*Tikkun* community"—including Susannah Heschel, a Dartmouth professor of Jewish studies, and such non-Jewish luminaries as Cornel West—placed a full-page ad in the *New York Times* in which, in classic anti-Semitic form, either Ariel Sharon or one of his "supporters" was presented in a cartoon caricature as a hook-nosed, evil-looking Jew, the state of Israel was characterized as a "Pharaoh," and Israeli soldiers were likened to Nazis blindly "following orders."[90] Earlier, Lerner was alone among Jewish public figures in allying himself with Louis Farrakhan to support Congresswoman Cynthia McKinney, declaring that "pro-Sharon forces have targeted this African-American Democrat for defeat."[91] Lerner has also organized conferences featuring such speakers as Paul McCloskey, a former congressman who has made appearances (together with David Irving) at conferences organized by the Institute for Historical Review, the California-based Holocaust-denial organization. At a recent *Tikkun*-sponsored gathering, McCloskey spoke out against the "most powerful lobby that this country has ever seen," i.e., the Jewish lobby, which he said has "pledged itself to a strong Israel, right or wrong, and [seeks] to intimidate…Jews that dare to criticize or speak out against the policies of the Israeli government."[92] Lerner did not demur.

To another Jew of this stripe, Marc Ellis, a professor of Jewish studies at Baylor University in Texas, "helicopter gunships" have become Judaism's central symbol, "as central to Jewish life as the Torah once was."[93] Given the Nazi-like behavior of the Israelis and their "relentlessly expanding state," Ellis believes that Palestinians are amply justified in "experiencing Jews in reality as aggressors and murderers." When Palestinians, he writes, "speak of 'the Jews' in a tone of disgust, they…tell a *truth* about my people's return that *no argument can dismiss*" (emphasis added).[94] To Daniel Boyarin, a leading academic figure in Jewish studies in the United States, Ehud Barak—the Israeli prime minister who made the most far-reaching concessions to the Palestinians in the history of the Arab-Israeli conflict—"is a violent man, a racist and a liar."[95] No less seething is Susannah Heschel, whose father, Abraham Joshua Heschel, was a prominent Jewish theologian of the twentieth century and an apostle of nonviolence; for the daughter, however, "there is ruthlessness in Israeli actions that leaves *no room for radical nonviolence*" (emphasis added). While this does not mean Israel should be wiped from the map, she grants, it needs to be transformed as thoroughly as was Nazi

Germany, another "profoundly racist state" toward which "our goal was to defeat its racism, not its existence."[96]*

❖

Small though their numbers may be, and as unrepresentative of the larger Jewish community as a Johannes Pfefferkorn or a Theobald of Cambridge, the cumulative impact of such extremists is enormous, both in the United States and around the world. It is one thing when a crackpot like David Duke denounces Israel and "worldwide Jewish Supremacism" in perfervid terms. Duke's words have been distributed widely in the Arab world, but in the West they resonate only in certain narrowly constricted circles. It is another thing, however, when similar ideas are voiced by Jewish activists and Jewish professors at leading American, European and Israeli universities. Such "renegade" Jews play a critical role today in legitimizing the hatred that, coming from non-Jewish voices, might seem unfit for discussion in polite company.

This is something that the anti-Semites themselves well understand. In its recruitment materials, Adam Shapiro's International Solidarity Movement stresses that "we particularly invite Jewish people to join," the reason being that "It is much more easy for Jewish people to enter Israel and more embarrassing for the Israeli government to deport Jews, making our Jewish contingent extremely valuable."[97] In the same vein, Patrick Buchanan is delighted to cite Harvard's Stanley Hoffmann, for it is "Hoffmann himself," he says, who has fingered a group of Jews shaping U.S. policy in accordance with their exclusive concern for Israel.[98] If a Jew like Hoffmann can openly level the charge of disloyalty at Wolfowitz, Perle and Feith, Buchanan is implicitly asserting, so can I.

The same psychology is evident in the alacrity with which

---

*Susannah Heschel is nothing if not incoherent. In this same essay, she also attacks left-wing anti-Semitism and those who call Israel racist, thereby managing inadvertently to condemn herself as well. *Tikkun,* May, 2003.

a whole host of non-Jewish bashers of Israel use the words of their Jewish friends to insulate themselves from the charge of anti-Semitism. Thus the black activist professor Cornel West declares he is proud to be associated with Louis Farrakhan because standing with him is Susannah Heschel, one of a number of "Jewish progressives...who will side with us" against the Jewish establishment.[99] "Because he is Jewish," the *Irish Times* reports with barely suppressed glee, "[Norman] Finkelstein gets away with the kind of language others would never be allowed to use. He accuses Jewish organizations, for example, of conducting themselves 'like a caricature from *Der Stuermer,*' the notorious Jew-baiting magazine of the Nazis."[100] To the Egyptian weekly *Al-Ahram,* Noam Chomsky's very existence is almost enough to prove that the sole purpose of the Oslo peace process was to mask "an American-Israeli project to dominate the region and liquidate the Palestinians as a people."[101] To Desmond Tutu, the South African churchman and anti-apartheid campaigner, who believes that the United States is governed by an irresistibly powerful "Jewish lobby," the writings of Marc Ellis provide "a vital contribution to solving one of the few remaining intractable problems of our time." To the late Edward Said, Ellis was "a brilliant writer, a deeply thoughtful and courageous mind."[102] To Christopher Hitchens, the prolific left-wing journalist who has had second thoughts about many but not all of his old causes, Israel Shahak was a "great and serious man."[103]

The barriers that have kept a poisonous idea in check in the decades since World War II are in the process of being swept away, and a coterie of preening left-wing Jews is in the vanguard of those doing the sweeping. In the whole shameful saga of this book, theirs is an especially sordid role.

❖

FIVE

Descent into Delusion

We have been tracing the course of an infection. So it's
only fair to ask: what sort of resistance has it encountered? If it cannot be cured, have measures at least been taken
to ameliorate or suppress its symptoms, or to prevent its further
spread?

In the Muslim world, where native antibodies to anti-
Semitism are pitifully lacking, there has been almost no
response at all; in the major and minor countries, the contagion
remains virulent. What's worse, the disease flows largely from
the top, from those nominally responsible for maintaining the
public health: government officials, educators, opinion-makers,
religious authorities and the like.

The plague is especially evident in the Arab and Muslim
Middle East, where many societies exhibit the signs of paralyz-
ing failure. Their elites are far too calcified, and far too
dependent on the precarious status quo, to risk dispensing with
the props by which they sustain themselves. Change for the
better, if it is to occur at all, will have to come from below, or be
instigated from the outside.

That is why Iraq is such an important case. Thanks to
American force of arms, the government of Saddam Hussein is
no more, and a major source of money, resources and inspiration for the haters has been cut off. Iraq's Arab and Muslim
neighbors are still absorbing the lessons of this watershed

event. Should the gargantuan task of reconstituting that country's civil society succeed, and should some measure of stable, democratic rule be established there, it cannot but set in motion a reconsideration of all the institutions in that part of the world that foster tyranny, among whose instruments is the propagation of hatred toward Jews.

There have been tentative signs of such a rethinking in some countries: harbingers, perhaps, of Gorbachev-like "reforms" from above, intended to mend what are perceived as minor flaws without toppling the entire dilapidated edifice. In a series of articles in *Al-Ahram,* for example, Osama al-Baz, a leading political adviser to Egyptian president Hosni Mubarak, has warned his countrymen that they are in danger of being blinded by Arab writers who draw on "racist" Nazi concepts and imagery to attack Jews. Al-Baz wrote in one of his articles that "Jews were exposed to the most brutal mass slaughters by Hitler and I wonder how can some Arab writers and politicians back his Nazi movement."[1] On the wider political front, as we have already seen, the beginnings of serious self-criticism (albeit tempered by ritual denunciations of Israel) are to be discerned in the *Arab Human Development Report.* And throughout this region of the world there are certainly many individuals who, though silent, are eager for change. But "silent" is the operative word. Today, a writer like al-Baz is still a soloist, and a carefully restrained one at that. For the most part, especially when it comes to the Jews, the chorus continues to intone a very different refrain.

❖

The democratic world presents a more complex picture, but also a more depressing one. Jewish organizations in Europe have mobilized to bring public attention to the rising tide of physical and verbal violence and to call for a governmental response. In the wake of September 11, individual law enforcement agencies among the European powers have also begun to focus on the problem of Muslim extremists, and to deal more harshly with perpetrators of "spontaneous" violence against

Jews. The member states of the Organization for Security and Cooperation in Europe, the largest collective-security body on the continent, have identified European anti-Semitism as a threat to the rule of law.

But the response has by no means been adequate or effective. In the world of politics, European opinion is heavily colored by new demographic realities. France, with the largest Muslim influx, represents the future, and politicians there have been quick to accommodate to their country's changing complexion. In *Le Monde,* the French socialist leader Pascal Boniface published an open "Letter to an Israeli Friend" whose real audience was clearly meant to be French Jews. The Arab population of France, Boniface stressed, "will be a counter-weight [to the Jewish community], and it will soon be numerically preponderant, if it is not already." Therefore, he warned, if the Jews wish to avoid unpleasant consequences (which Boniface declined to specify), they would be well advised not to "permit too much impunity to the Israeli government."[2]

The menacing words of a Boniface at least have the excuse of naked political calculation. More troubling has been a widespread refusal to see things as they are or to call them by their proper name. So eager are some public officials to wish away the problem of anti-Semitism that, in effect, they dematerialize it. In Kiev, where youths attacked the city's central synagogue chanting "Kill the kikes," the police insisted that this was an instance not of anti-Semitism but of "soccer-related hooliganism."[3] And in France, the country that has witnessed the worst outbreak of European anti-Semitism since World War II, President Chirac has declared that "There is no anti-Semitism and [there are] no anti-Semites."[4]

But public officials are hardly the worst offenders when it comes to denying or excusing violence and incitement to violence. Truly scandalous has been the complicity of Europe's "enlightened" and "progressive" opinion-makers in justifying anti-Jewish agitation. In a lengthy and impassioned indictment of her own colleagues, the Italian writer Oriana Fallaci spoke out against the pernicious role played by the European media in promoting the cause of Palestinian terrorism:

> I find it shameful...that state-run television stations [in Italy] contribute to the resurgent anti-Semitism, crying only over Palestinian deaths while playing down Israeli deaths, glossing over them in unwilling tones. I find it shameful that in their debates they host with much deference the scoundrels with turbans or kefiyahs who yesterday sang hymns to the slaughter in New York and today sing hymns to the slaughters in Jerusalem, in Haifa, in Netanya, in Tel Aviv....[5]

But although her book on this subject, *The Rage and the Pride,* was a European bestseller, Fallaci remains among the few exceptions; the "shameful" pattern she describes remains the rule.

❖

This brings us to another facet of the nonresponse to anti-Semitism—and at this point our discussion can broaden out to include the United States. Just as there is an intellectual disease called Holocaust denial, there is a related pathology that might be called anti-Semitism denial. And just as Holocaust denial covers a spectrum, from outright crackpots who hold that no genocide took place at all to revisionist "historians" who concede Nazi intentions but minimize the numbers of the murdered, so too does anti-Semitism denial come in a variety of shades and hues.

Among the most avid deniers are the anti-Semites themselves. The Reverend Louis Farrakhan, for example, who has called Judaism a "gutter religion," is not, by his own lights, anti-Semitic in the least: "Let me say, for the record, I am not now, nor have I ever been, a hater or disrespecter of the Jewish people. My disagreement is with aspects of that community who seek to control black thought, black expression, black talent, black politics, black religion, black people."[6] Notice the two-step maneuver: a denial of anti-Semitism followed by a renewed and amplified assault on the Jews. A virtuoso of the same trick is Patrick Buchanan, who has explained that his magazine does not attack neoconservatives "because they are Jewish.... We attack them because their warmongering threatens our country, even as it finds a reliable echo in Ariel Sharon."[7]

The preferred technique of many deniers is to charge those who *raise* the issue of anti-Semitism with attempting to end honest debate or to stifle any criticism of Israel. Noted communitarian thinker Amitai Etzioni writes: "It is completely uncalled for to label as anti-Semitic the criticisms of the Sharon government, and of current Israeli policy regarding the West Bank and Gaza Strip."[8] (To which one might reply: It depends on the criticism. Many such criticisms are legitimate. Many others, however, knowingly based on unabashed exaggerations and outright lies, are of the same stripe as the "criticism" that Jews drain the blood of children or a hundred similar libels.) Three of Israel's recent prime ministers have been "mass murderers," writes Joel Kovel, complaining in the next breath that to point out this "fact" is to invite being "called 'self-hating' and 'anti-Semitic.'"[9] (One cannot imagine why.) "If you say anything at all against the Jews," laments Malaysia's Mahathir Mohamad, "you are accused of being anti-Semitic."[10] By such means are the most extravagant and unfounded charges insulated from condemnation.

Another well-honed technique is to define anti-Semitism so narrowly as to limit it to the Nazi Holocaust and practically nothing else. Today, observes the theologian Emil Fackenheim of this gambit, "unless someone actually wants to kill Jews, he does not qualify as an anti-Semite."[11] And in some respectable quarters, even the frank expression of such a desire to kill Jews does not qualify. For Amitai Etzioni, "calls to destroy Israel, or to throw it into the Mediterranean Sea…are not evidence of hatred of Jews" but rather merely "reflect a quarrel with the state of Israel."[12] When anti-Israel demonstrators in France carried posters reading "Death to Jews," the *New York Times* seemed in genuine doubt about what such "ferocious" language signified: did it "mark a recrudescence of that most ugly of Western diseases, anti-Semitism? Or [was] it legitimate, if crude, criticism of a nation's policies? Where does one draw the line?"[13]

To such tortuous lengths have some gone in order to turn a blind eye to the obvious.

❖

As these examples attest, anti-Semitism today, whether crude or sophisticated, very often travels under an alias, and the most ubiquitous such alias is anti-Zionism. The legions of the world's anti-Zionists purport to be neutral in their attitude toward Jews and Judaism, opposing only the founding of Israel, or its continued existence, or its policies. But the quality of their obsession with the malefactions of the Jewish state alone among all the member states of the world community, and the extremity of their denunciations of it, show what is under the mask.

A vivid example of how far things have gone in this direction could be seen in the United Nations World Conference Against Racism held in Durban, South Africa, in 2001. Ostensibly devoted to combating prejudice of all kinds, the conference wound up formally condemning the only democracy in the Middle East, justifying violence and terrorism against it, and in effect calling for its destruction. A resolution containing a plethora of anti-Zionist *and* anti-Semitic formulations, drafted in a preparatory meeting held in—of all countries—Iran, lambasted Israel for engaging in the "Zionist practices" of "apartheid" and "racial discrimination." Far harsher language was employed in the accompanying speeches, with Israel portrayed as the central locus of evil in the contemporary world and a number of delegates advancing the proposition that the Nazi Holocaust was actually nothing more than, in the words of the Syrian representative, "a Jewish lie."[14]

In the conference hall where these proceedings were under way, openly anti-Jewish literature was being distributed; in one leaflet, a resurrected Hitler was pictured saying, "If I had not lost, Israel would not exist today."[15] Threats of physi-

146

cal violence greeted delegates who had the temerity to wear skullcaps or any other garb identifying themselves as Jewish. The gathering, in the accurate words of Hillel Halkin, was "the largest and best-publicized international anti-Semitic rally in history."[16]

More than a century ago, the French socialist thinker Pierre Proudhon wrote that "the Jew is the "enemy of mankind," a race that "poisons everything, by butting in everywhere, without ever merging with any people."[17] Precisely the same indictment was leveled at Israel in Durban and is leveled at Israel today: a state castigated as an enemy of mankind for no other reason than that it stubbornly refuses to give up its identity and disappear. If, for Proudhon, the "solution" to this enduring Jewish problem was to expel the Jews from France or to "exterminate" (!) them—"except," he graciously allowed, "for individuals married to Frenchwomen"[18]—a similar, almost genocidal impulse lurks behind those seething with hatred for the Jewish state.

In short, the state of Israel, in the mordant phrase of the historian Jacob Talmon, has been transformed into "the 'Jew' of the nations." As such, it makes its appearance on the stage of world affairs to play a variety of assigned and time-dishonored roles: as a pariah; as a supernaturally powerful and crafty entity; as the headquarters of a global conspiracy manipulating events everywhere; as a malign force directly responsible for the world's ineradicable ills. Like the hapless Jews of Christian Europe, the Jewish state stands accused of a variety of fantastical crimes for which it must, in turn, be brutally punished.

❖

To its everlasting credit, the Bush administration declined to send a representative to participate in the anti-Semitic circus at Durban, but thereby provoked yet another round of denial. The liberal human rights group Amnesty International, while entirely ignoring the blatant anti-Semitism of the conference resolution, denounced the United States government for its "disgraceful, reprehensible, and morally indefensible" decision not to participate.[19] Another such group, Human Rights Watch, did bring itself to criticize the Durban resolution—for what it euphemistically labeled "intemperate language"—before proceeding to condemn Israel for alleged "serious abuses."[20]

The biases of liberal-to-Left organizations like Human Rights Watch and Amnesty International are longstanding and have been amply documented. Both have issued numerous one-sided reports in which, through the use of double standards and selective evidence, democratic Israel is made to appear a flagrant violator of human rights while the closed and aggressive tyrannies that are Israel's neighbors are given a pass. But these organizations are not alone in either ignoring or minimizing the dimensions of today's anti-Semitism. They swim in a wider current, one that even includes friends and supporters of Israel.

To Leon Wieseltier, literary editor of the *New Republic* and a devoted proponent of the Oslo peace process, talk of a resurgent anti-Semitism is both inapposite and dangerous, a case of fretfulness run amok. The Jewish community in the United States, Wieseltier wrote in the spring of 2002, has become "sunk in excitability, in the imagination of disaster." In the face of a few anti-Semitic incidents in Europe and a few more terrorist attacks in Israel, there has been "a loss of intellectual control. Death is at every Jewish door. Fear is wild. Reason is derailed."[21]

Adducing no real evidence to support his portrait of a Jewish community in panic, Wieseltier at least was frank about why it was so urgent to remind readers that "Hitler is dead," as the title of his essay declared, and that it was mere "theology" to imagine otherwise. For if the Arab attitude toward Israel does partake of a truly genocidal hatred, then the prospects of a negotiated peace settlement in which Israel would make tangible concessions of territory and security in exchange for Arab proclamations of good will—that is, the kind of peace settlement to which he himself had been publicly committed for so long—are doomed. It was this intricate chain of considerations that apparently led Wieseltier to dismiss fears of a new wave of anti-Semitism as nothing more than "ethnic panic."[22]

More extreme than Wieseltier is Tony Judt, a professor of history at New York University, a regular contributor to the *New York Review of Books* and an unbending Jewish critic of Israel—the very idea of which, he contends, is an "anachronism" in today's "world of individual rights, open frontiers, and international law."[23] To Judt, the claim "that Europe is awash in anti-Semitism" is nothing more than a pernicious "Europhobic myth," a myth exploited by its proponents to discredit a "widespread European criticism of Israel" that is itself perfectly justified. As for the spate of violent attacks on Jewish symbols and European Jews themselves, these can be given to less inflammatory interpretations: "Measured by everything from graffiti to violent assaults," Judt writes, "anti-Semitism has indeed been on the increase in some European countries in recent years; but then so it has in America," and there is "no evidence to suggest it is more widespread in Europe than in the U.S."[24]

Even if Judt had gotten the facts correct—in actuality, the violence in Europe has greatly exceeded levels in the United States—one would think that a rising number of incidents in both Europe and the United States would be cause for greater alarm, not less. But that aside, what Judt really wants to explain to his readers is the *reason* for the increase in European anti-Semitism. It is, in a word, Israel. In contrast to Americans, Europeans "are more likely to blame Israel than Palestinians for the present morass in the Middle East." Far from reflecting any prejudice, however, this anti-Israel judgment is a proper one, and precisely what one should expect given the fact that Europeans are so much better *informed* than we: "the European press, radio, and television provide a fuller and fairer coverage of events in the Middle East than is available to most Americans."[25]

If, by "fuller and fairer," Judt has in mind the stream of anti-Israel propaganda and outright anti-Semitic lies that pass for much of the "coverage" of the Middle East in the European media, then he is right. That this is what he indeed has in mind is suggested by the fact that he himself regards Israel as a "colonial power," and has called for its dissolution and the formation of a "binational" state in its place.[26] It's no wonder that he finds so much to admire in the work of the European media, whose prejudices neatly confirm his own.

In the sophisticated gyrations of Tony Judt we would seem to have another example of a type we encountered earlier: a man so anxious to deflect from himself the poisonous arrows coming at his fellow Jews that he must publicly disown an entire Jewish collectivity. That he does so at a moment of great extremity, when the members of that collectivity live under daily mortal threat, puts him in a long and unsavory line of individuals whose motives he himself reveals in astonishingly candid words. Israel, Judt complains, is holding the world's Jews—i.e., him—"hostage for its own actions." Although Jews in the Diaspora—i.e., he—"cannot influence Israeli policies... The behavior of a self-described Jewish state affects the way everyone else looks at Jews"—i.e., him.[27] Seldom has the psychology of contemporary Jewish self-hatred been given more lucid expression.

❖

If there are those who minimize, ignore or deny anti-Semitism, what is the true picture? How bad is today's situation? Are we approaching a 1933 or a 1939? How, in the end, are we to draw the balance sheet?

In the Islamic world, societies teetering on the brink of social and political collapse, unable or unwilling to come to terms with modernity, have proved easy prey to extremist creeds and ideologies. For the regimes ruling these societies, anti-Semitism has served as an especially powerful and convenient tool, a means of blaming near or distant others for profound problems whose cause and cure lie at home. Adding to the combustibility is the fact that some of these societies are staggeringly poor while others, disposing of immense resources, use them in part to foment anti-Semitic hatred in the poverty-stricken ones.

If the danger is great, it is augmented by the determination of some of the most badly infected countries to acquire weapons of mass destruction and the missiles to deliver them. Pakistan already has what it calls the "Islamic bomb." For the moment, its government seems capable of making rational choices, but Pakistan's governments have been regularly toppled by military coups. A major segment of the population is in the grip of radical Islam, and some leading nuclear scientists themselves have close ties to the most fanatical Muslims of Afghanistan and to al-Qaeda. If radical Islamists were ever to ascend to power in Pakistan, the prospect would loom of a transfer of nuclear weapons to the remnants of al-Qaeda or to other Islamic terrorists. This would pose an intolerable threat to India, to the United States and, of course, to Israel.

No less menacing is the peril posed by Iran. Tehran's ayatollahs have been engaged in a crash program to acquire nuclear weapons and are believed to be within two or three years of possessing them—unless they purchase them today or tomorrow or next month from the nuclear-armed rogue state of North Korea. We do not know with any precision how far Iran has progressed, but we do know that Iran already has the means—that is, the missiles—to deliver nuclear weapons and has flaunted these means in military parades with banners reading "Israel Should Be Wiped from the Map."[28]

True, Israel has nuclear weapons of its own; in Leon Wieseltier's reassuring words, "the Jews have a spectacular deterrent."[29] But there are grounds for doubting that Iran will be deterred. Iran's "moderate" former president, the Ayatollah Ali Akbar Hashemi Rafsanjani, has publicly reasoned as follows: "the use of an atomic bomb against Israel would totally destroy Israel, while [the same] against the Islamic world would only cause damage."[30] Nor are fanatics turned aside by the thought of self-immolation. According to Ayatollah Yusuf Sani'i, a senior member of Iran's ruling council, "All religious persons and Islamic leaders must encourage and teach the value of the deed of suicide. We ask God to illuminate all Muslims and to seat all the fallen in the first row."[31]

Just as Israel now confronts individual suicide bombers eager to give up their own lives in the hope of taking large numbers of Israeli civilians with them, we may yet see the emergence of suicide states, willing to sacrifice substantial portions of their own populace for the sake of destroying the Jews. Hitler may be dead, but the desire to rid the world of Jews remains alive, and in the Middle East it has been given fresh impetus by the increasing availability of instruments of mass murder. In the age of terrorism and weapons of mass destruction, the last and most terrible chapter of the Islamist brand of anti-Semitism may remain to be written.

❖

In the stable and democratic West, the course of anti-Semitism is more obscure. We are dealing, after all, with a profoundly irrational creed—the "socialism of fools," as the socialist August Bebel famously characterized it—and its ways are recalcitrant to analysis and prediction. If anti-Semitism waned in the decades after World War II, we can now understand that it lingered in various forms not far beneath the surface: a set of prejudices and hatreds ingrained in the Western consciousness over millennia and all too readily summoned forth, sometimes in response to concrete circumstances and events, sometimes with apparent capriciousness.

Today's virulent outbreak in Europe and (to a much lesser extent) in the United States does appear to be an epiphenomenon of the Arab-Israel conflict. Anti-Semitism unquestionably intensified greatly on both continents with the eruption of the second intifada in the autumn of 2000, and it seems to have gained additional momentum as the continuing Israeli-Palestinian crisis moves from peak to peak. If, then, Israel succeeds in thwarting or turning aside the Arab determination to destroy it, will the rhetoric abate, and will explicit anti-Semitism diminish?

It could happen. Historically, the perception of Jewish

weakness has always fed the appetite of anti-Jewish aggression; by the same token, that aggression can be contained by a sufficient show of strength and determination. Whatever the expectations of their assailants, the Jewish people have so far proved themselves both strong and amazingly determined. But even if the anti-Semitic upsurge is in fact linked to the battles of the Middle East, and even if these battles subside, trends wholly separate from the Israel-Palestine conflict suggest that what has been ignited may not so easily burn out.

One particularly alarming sign—a straw in the wind?—is the open speculation that has suddenly sprung up in the most respectable quarters about the possibility of a world without Israel. That a Hamas spokesman like the late Ismail Abu Shanab should contemplate the extinction of the Jewish state is understandable; that he should have felt comfortable in talking about it publicly—"There are," he amiably explained to the *New York Times,* "a lot of open areas in the United States that could absorb the Jews"—tells us a good deal about what has come to be considered permissible discourse in the presence of Western reporters.[32] But then, as we have seen, the well-known British literary figures Tom Paulin and A. N. Wilson have followed close behind, and similar thoughts, suitably qualified, have even appeared under the bylines of avowed friends of the Jewish state here at home. As one of them, the theologian Richard John Neuhaus, has written, to "wish that Israel 'would cease to exist' is…not necessarily a wish to destroy the Jews, since one might at the same time hope that the minority of the world's Jews living in Israel would find a secure home elsewhere, notably in the U.S."[33]

Neuhaus, it must be stressed, disclaims any such sentiment himself. But others, unfastidiously and without any disclaimers, have called for the dismantlement of the state of Israel—as if it were a perfectly ordinary and reasonable prospect for a thriving democracy of nearly five million Jews voluntarily to disappear. "Trying to create a small Jewish state in a sea of Muslims was a 20th-century mistake," explains the syndicated columnist Paul Craig Roberts. "Why not recognize the mistake, evacuate the Jews, leave the Muslims to themselves, and focus on saving our own country?"[34]

These are, at best, rationalizations—evidence, perhaps, of the degree to which the fantastic thinking of the anti-Semites has infected otherwise balanced minds. Even if we credit the seriousness of their authors' intentions, it is impossible to conceive of the circumstances under which such outlandish scenarios might successfully play themselves out. In 1975, the United States did not exactly spread a welcome mat for its allies in Cambodia whom it had pledged but failed to defend from Communist aggression; in short order, they were slaughtered by the millions. An older and even more relevant episode took place when, in the 1930s and 1940s, Washington did its best to keep Jewish refugees from Nazism out—on one notorious occasion, in 1939, refusing admission to those aboard the steamship *St. Louis* and forcing the ship back to Europe, where most of the 937 passengers met their deaths.

One might hope that things would be different in our enlightened age. But this hope is a reed that splinters in an instant against the practical obstacles in the way of rapidly ferrying five million Jews to safety from the Middle East. Exactly how would such a mass evacuation take place? To ask the question is to answer it. We should confess to ourselves the likelier truth: if Israel "would cease to exist," so, inevitably, would most of its Jews. To "wish that Israel would 'cease to exist'" is, in effect, to wish for the mass extinction of its Jews. If that is not an anti-Semitic sentiment, what is?

An even more alarming sign of the times has cropped up repeatedly in the pages of this book: the rising status of the forgery that is the *Protocols of the Elders of Zion*. Notwithstanding its manifest incoherence and even absurdity, this document, composed at the close of the nineteenth century by the czarist secret police, has surfaced again and again since that time, fueling hatred of Jews in every period of social and political tumult. Today, a century after it was written, the *Protocols* is being peddled to an audience vaster than any of its authors could have imagined, staged in television productions for millions of viewers in the Arab world, sold in Europe in the bookstores of the radical Left and Right, and circulated on the Internet in practically every language, major and minor.

Here in the United States, this same malevolent volume is hawked on street corners by black Muslim followers of Louis Farrakhan, excerpted and serialized in the Arab-language press, and distributed by "anti-Zionist" activists on college campuses. The warning it sounds—about a covert and sinister Jewish manipulation of world events—has now entered mainstream opinion in the form of ritual denunciations of the Wolfowitz-Perle-Feith troika.

In the decades before World War II, the *Protocols,* together with a mass of other anti-Semitic writings, including *Mein Kampf* and beyond, helped prepare the intellectual and cultural groundwork for the catastrophe that followed. Today, the same and similar material is once again ubiquitous, accompanied and amplified by ceaseless imprecations on the part of the international Left against Israel and its supporters. By this route has the disease of anti-Semitism returned to infect our politics and our culture, leaping from one host body to another and mutating into ever more grotesque forms.

Great shocks, as we know from the last century, can produce political flux beyond all foresight. In recent years the world has been subjected to a series of such shocks, September 11 being the greatest of them. More may be on the way, and where their repercussions will end no one can yet know. But the concomitant and hardly coincidental revival of the ancient fear and hatred known as anti-Semitism must make one tremble. So too must the indifference and denial that have greeted its resurgence.

The barriers around my office in New York are not a sign of "ethnic panic." They are a sign of realism in the face of danger. If the danger is growing, one reason is that, as those physical barriers have gone up, other and even more necessary barriers—political, moral and intellectual—have fallen with frightening rapidity. A taboo thought to have been firmly fixed in place a half-century after the greatest paroxysm of violence and hatred in the history of the world is no more.

In the concluding words of *Warrant for Genocide,* his 1966 study of European anti-Semitism in the years before World War II, the historian Norman Cohn summarized the causes of twentieth-century anti-Semitism and its significance for the destiny of nations:

> A grossly delusional view of the world, based on infantile fears and hatreds, was able to find expression in murder and torture beyond all imagining. It is a case-history in collective psychopathology, and its deepest implications reach far beyond anti-Semitism and the fate of the Jews.[35]

Those words remain relevant today.

ACKNOWLEDGMENTS

I am indebted to Cyma Horowitz and Michelle Anish, librarians of the American Jewish Committee, for their invaluable assistance in the preparation of this book, and to the American Jewish Committee for maintaining such an excellent library on its premises. The American Jewish Committee's Lawrence Grossman generously provided me with an advance look at selections from the *American Jewish Year Book,* of which he serves as editor. I extend heartfelt thanks to my publisher, Peter Collier of Encounter Books, for his spirited and highly professional guidance from the project's inception to its end. I am heavily indebted to Roger Hertog for his encouragement and advice. My colleagues at *Commentary,* Gary Rosen and Benjamin Balint, were helpful in ways too numerous to spell out here; I am particularly grateful to the indispensable Rachel Z. Friedman for her expert assistance with the notes.

Several friends—Karen Lehrman, Adam Schulman, Dianne Sehler, Sarah May Stern, Laura Weeks and especially Joan Richards—helped me at various junctures in various ways, small and great, that I am happy to be able to acknowledge. The wise direction of Samuel C. Klagsbrun and Susanna L. Neumann helped to preserve my sanity under the strain of a tight deadline and other pressures. Edward and Marilyn Rothstein provided me with a second home and exhibited a generosity too profound to recognize adequately in print.

I have a special debt to Norman Podhoretz, whose thinking on the question of anti-Semitism, as on so many other issues, has been a lodestar. As editor of *Commentary* from 1960 to 1995, he also published important essays by Ruth R. Wisse, Léon Poliakov, Milton Himmelfarb, Robert S. Wistrich and a number of other writers whose thinking has heavily influenced my own.

I thank my sister, Miriam DiMaio, for her unstinting support and encouragement. Thanks for unstinting support and inspiration also go to my mother, Laure Lehrer, and my aunt, Jeanne Jonas—both of whom, it is pertinent to mention, arrived in the United States in 1943 after a harrowing escape from Nazi Germany and occupied France. My late father, Herman Schoenfeld, bequeathed me a priceless intellectual heritage for which there are no sufficient thanks. Finally, I thank my three beautiful daughters—Esther, Shoshana and Ruth—for their love. May they live in a world free of anti-Semitism.

NOTES

PART ONE: Warning Signs
1 Sebastian Haffner, *Defying Hitler* (New York, 2002), p. 145.
2 Naomi W. Cohen, *Not Free to Desist: The American Jewish Committee, 1906–1966* (Philadelphia, 1972), p. 147.

PART TWO: The Islamic Strain
1 Mahathir Mohamad, *The Malay Dilemma* (Singapore, 1970); in Lindsay Shanson, "Malaysia's Orangutan Plot," *Jerusalem Report,* June 6, 1991.
2 Anti-Defamation League Press Release, October 13, 1997.
3 Shanson, "Malaysia's Orangutan Plot."
4 Michael Kamber, "The Chosen One," *Village Voice,* March 5, 2002.
5 Alex Alexiev, "The Pakistani Time Bomb," *Commentary,* March 2003.
6 Susan Sachs, "10 Jews Convicted by Iranian Court in Espionage Case," *New York Times,* July 2, 2000.
7 *Tehran Times,* February 1, 2001; in *Anti-Semitism Worldwide, 2000/1,* compiled by the Stephen Roth Institute for the Study of Contemporary Anti-Semitism and Racism at Tel Aviv University (Tel Aviv, 2001), p. 252.
8 In *Anti-Semitism Worldwide, 2000/1,* p. 250.
9 Introduction to the *Protocols of the Elders of Zion,* pub-

lished by the government of Iran; translated by MEMRI, cited in Special Dispatch Series no. 98, June 7, 2000.

10 Ibid.

11 Ibid.

12 Fatma Abdallah Mahmoud, "Accursed Forever and Ever," *Al-Akhbar,* April 29, 2002; translated by MEMRI, cited in Special Dispatch Series no. 375, May 3, 2002.

13 Ahmad Ragab, "Half a Word," *Al-Akhbar,* April 18, 2001; translated by MEMRI, cited in Special Dispatch Series no. 208, April 20, 2001.

14 Mahmoud, "Accursed Forever and Ever"; translated by MEMRI.

15 Mohamed Hasanein Heikal, Foreword to the Arabic edition of Garaudy's *The Founding Myths of Modern Israel* (Cairo, 1998); translated by Abdullah M. Sindi and printed in *Journal for Historical Review,* vol. 19, no. 6, November/December 2000.

16 Dr. Mahmoud al-Said al-Kurdi, "The Last Scene in the Life of Father Toma!!—A Tele-drama for the Arab Summit in Amman!" *Al-Akhbar,* March 25, 2001; translated by MEMRI, cited in Special Dispatch Series no. 201, April 2, 2001.

17 *Roz al-Youssuf,* November 17, 2001; translated by MEMRI, cited in Special Dispatch Series no. 309, December 6, 2001.

18 Salah al-Din Hilmi, "The Jews Are Bloodsuckers and Will Yet Conquer America," *Akher Sa'a,* January 9, 2002; translated by MEMRI, cited in Special Dispatch Series no. 339, January 31, 2002.

19 Dr. Husniya Hassan Moussa, "The Germ War," *Al-'ilm,* November 2001; translated by MEMRI, cited in Special Dispatch Series no. 322, December 28, 2001.

20 "Battle Looms for Credit over Anti-Israel Lyrics," *Los Angeles Times,* May 9, 2001.

21 Sudarsan Raghavan, "Artists Fuel Arab Rage against U.S. and Israel," *Philadelphia Inquirer,* March 12, 2001.

22 Dr. Umayma Ahmad al-Jalahma, "The Jewish Holiday of

Purim," *Al-Riyadh,* March 10, 2002; translated by MEMRI, cited in Special Dispatch Series no. 354, March 13, 2002.

23 Dr. Muhammad bin S'ad al-Shwey'ir, *Al-Jazirah,* June 7, 2002; translated by MEMRI, cited in Special Dispatch Series no. 421, September 19, 2002.

24 "Raw Data: Interview with Muslim Girl," *FOX News,* June 15, 2002.

25 "The Opposite Direction," Al-Jazeera TV, January 22, 2002; translated by MEMRI, cited in Special Dispatch Series no. 343, February 8, 2002. *Jihad, Jews, and Anti-Semitism in Syrian School Texts,* B'nai B'rith International, pp. 15–16; based on "Jews, Zionism, and Syrian School Textbooks," a report by the Center for Monitoring the Impact of Peace, June 2001.

26 *Jihad, Jews, and Anti-Semitism in Syrian School Texts,* pp. 15–16.

27 Mustafa Tlass, Introduction to *The Matzah of Zion* (Damascus, 1986); translated by MEMRI, cited in MEMRI Inquiry and Analysis Series no. 99, June 27, 2002.

28 *Al-Hayat,* October 21, 2002; translated from the Arabic by MEMRI, cited in Special Dispatch Series no. 432, October 22, 2002.

29 Naser Ahmad, "Reaching the Congress," *Al-Hayat al-Jadida,* November 7, 1998; translated by MEMRI, cited in Special Dispatch Series no. 12, November 13, 1998.

30 Seif 'Ali al-Jarwan, "Jewish Control of the World Media," *Al-Hayat al-Jadida,* July 2, 1998; translated by MEMRI, cited in Special Dispatch Series no. 1, July 15, 1998.

31 Itamar Marcus, *The Palestinian Authority School Books and Teacher's Guide,* 2nd ed., Report P-01-03 of the Center for Monitoring the Impact of Peace, March 2001, p. 6.

32 "Interview with 'Ikrima Sabri," *Die Welt,* January, 17, 2001; translated by MEMRI, cited in Special Dispatch Series no. 182, January 24, 2001.

33 Sheikh Ibrahim Madhi on official Palestinian Authority television, April 12, 2002; translated by MEMRI, cited in Special Dispatch Series no. 370, April 17, 2002.

34 Dr. Alhmad Abu Halabiya on Palestinian Authority television; translated by MEMRI, cited in Special Dispatch Series no. 138, October 13, 2000.

35 Mark Lavie, "Abbas Becomes First Palestinian Premier in Shadow of Looming Iraq Conflict," Associated Press, March 19, 2003.

36 James Bennet and John Kifner, "6 Men Who Could Be Contenders to Lead the Palestinians if Arafat Goes," *New York Times,* June 14, 2002.

37 *Al-Istiqlal,* February 26, 1999; translated by MEMRI, cited in Special Dispatch Series no. 26, March 5, 1999.

38 Excerpts from a speech by Hizbollah Secretary-General Hassan Nasrallah, April 9, 2000; available on the Israel Ministry of Foreign Affairs website, www.israel.org/mfa.

39 "Over 3 Million Moroccans Show Support for Palestinians," Panafrican News Agency Daily News Wire, April 17, 2000.

40 Bernard Lewis, *Semites and Anti-Semites* (New York, 1987), p. 256.

41 Ibid.

42 Ibid.

43 Ibid.

44 Ibid.

45 The Interim Agreement (Oslo 2) of September 28, 1995 (Article XXII).

46 *The Arab Human Development Report 2002,* published by the United Nations Development Program, Regional Bureau for Arab States, available online at http://www.undp.org.

47 Ibid., p. 5.

48 Ibid., p. 78.

49 Ibid., p. 9, p. 2.

50 Ibid., p. 2.

51 Ibid., pp. 8–9.

52 Ibid., p. 1.

53 Ibid., p. 2.

54 Ibid., p. 2.

55 Efraim Karsh, "What Occupation?" *Commentary,* July/ August 2002.

56 Ladan Boroumand and Roya Boroumand, "Terror, Islam, and Democracy," *Journal of Democracy,* vol. 13, no. 2 (2002): 5–20.

57 Dirk van Arkel, "Antisemitism in Austria," doctoral dissertation, University of Leiden, 1966; quoted in Léon Poliakov, *The History of Anti-Semitism,* trans. George Klim (New York, 1985), vol. 3, p. 17.

58 Raphael Patai, *The Arab Mind* (New York, 2002), pp. 53–54.

59 Ibid., p. 54.

60 Michael Oren, *Six Days of War: June 1967 and the Making of the Modern Middle East* (New York, 2002), p. 217.

61 Fouad Ajami, "Where Nuance Had Its Chance," *U.S. News & World Report,* August 5, 2002.

62 Ronald L. Nettler, *Past Trials and Present Tribulations: A Muslim Fundamentalist's View of the Jews* (Oxford, 1987), p. 7.

63 Ibid., p. 7.

64 Poliakov, *The History of Anti-Semitism,* vol. 1, p. 25.

65 Lewis, *Semites and Anti-Semites,* p. 122.

66 Ibid., p. 122.

67 Sylvia G. Haim, "Arabic Antisemitic Literature: Some Preliminary Notes," in *Jewish Social Studies,* vol. 17, no. 4 (1955): 307–12.

68 Lewis, *Semites and Anti-Semites,* p. 199.

69 From the mufti's Berlin radio broadcast, March 1, 1944, in Lukasz Hirszowicz, *The Third Reich and the Arab East,* trans. III Rzesza I Arabski Wschod (London, 1966), p. 311.

70 Quoted in a speech given by Farouk al-Shara, Syrian minister of foreign affairs, on October 30, 1991 at the Madrid Conference, translated by the Israel Ministry of Foreign Affairs, available online at www.israel.org/mfa.

71 "Assad Accused of Inflaming Religious Passions," Associated Press, May 7, 2001.

72 Mahdi Fadl Allah, *With Sayyid Qutb in His Political and Religious Thought* (Beirut, 1979), in Nettler, *Past Trials and Present Tribulations,* p. 25.

73 From Qutb's American letters. In Jonathan Raban, "Truly, Madly, Deeply Devout," *Guardian* (London), March 2, 2002.

74 Lawrence Wright, "The Man behind Bin Laden," *New Yorker,* September 16, 2002.

75 Sayyid Qutb, *Our Struggle with the Jews* (Saudi Arabia, 1970), p. 7; in the translation of this work by Nettler in *Past Trials and Present Tribulations,* p. 78. Words in brackets as in original.

76 Nettler, *Past Trials and Present Tribulations,* p. 75. Brackets as in original.

77 Ibid., pp. 76–77.

78 Ibid., p. 83.

79 Ibid., p. 85.

80 Ibid., pp. 86–87.

81 Ruhollah Khomeini, "Islamic Government," in *Islam in Transition: Muslim Perspectives,* ed. John Donohue and John Esposito (New York, 1982), pp. 314–15.

82 Excerpts from a speech by Hassan Nasrallah, April 9, 2000, available on the Israel Ministry of Foreign Affairs website, www.israel.org/mfa.

83 Fiamma Nirenstein, "How Suicide Bombers Are Made," *Commentary,* September 2001.

84 Quoted in Wolfgang Benz, *The Holocaust* (New York, 1999), p. 153.

85 Dr. Lufti Abd al-Azim, *Al-Ahram,* September 27, 1982; in Lewis, *Semites and Anti-Semites,* p. 195.

86 Barbara Demick, "Member of Palestinian Mob...Proudly Proclaims Murder," *Akron Beacon Journal,* October 14, 2000.

87 Deborah Sontag, "Whose Holy Land?" *New York Times,* October 13, 2000.

88 Mohammed Daraghmeh, "Palestinians Put on Gruesome Events in Exhibition Marking Anniversary of Uprising with Israel-Palestinians," Associated Press Worldstream, September 23, 2001.

89 Susan Sachs, "First of Iranian Spy Suspects Is Tried and Confesses on TV," *New York Times,* May 2, 2000.

90 Dennis Ross, "The Hidden Threat in the Middle East," *Wall Street Journal,* July 24, 2002.

91 Ali Akbar Hashemi Rafsanjani, Friday prayer sermon at Tehran University, December 14, 2001; translated by BBC Worldwide Monitoring, December 15, 2001.

92 Ian Fisher, "New Scrutiny of the Accused in a Terrorism Trial in Jordan," *New York Times,* October 14, 2001.

93 Jamal Halaby, "Military Court Sentences Millennium Terror Plot Defendant to Death," Associated Press, February 11, 2002.

94 "Shoe Bomb Suspect Says He Was Targeting Enemies of Islam, Court Documents Say," Associated Press, September 12, 2002.

95 "Sampling of Rants by Zacarias Moussaoui, the Only 9/11 Defendant," Agence France-Presse, July 25, 2002.

96 Jason Burke, "Terror Video Used to Lure UK Muslims; Mosque Recruitment Film Shows Bin Laden Slayings," *Observer* (London), January 27, 2002.

97 Dominic Kennedy, "Britain's Sheikh of Race Hate," *Times* (London), February 4, 2002.

98 Daniel Rubin and Michael Dorgan, "Brain behind Terrorist Plots Eludes Police to This Day," *Sun Herald,* September 11, 2002.

99 Peter Finn, "Hamburg's Cauldron of Terror; Within Cell of 7, Hatred of U.S. Grew and Sept. 11 Plot Evolved," *Washington Post,* September 11, 2002.

100 Ayman al-Zawahiri, *Knights under the Prophet's Banner,* originally printed in *Al-Sharq al-Awsat* (London); translated by the U.S. Foreign Broadcast Information Service, available online at www.fas.org.

101 John Miller interview with bin Laden, *ABC News,* May 28, 1998.

102 From a 1996 interview with Nida' al-Islam (Australia), in Yehudit Barsky, "Osama bin Laden and Al-Qa'ida," American Jewish Committee Briefing, September 13, 2001; available online at www.ajc.org.

103 Osama bin Laden, "Letter to the American People,"

printed in English in the *Observer* (London), November 24, 2002.

[104] John Miller interview with bin Laden, *ABC News,* May 28, 1998.

[105] Leslie Stahl interview with Ramzi Ahmed Yousef, *60 Minutes,* June 2, 2002.

[106] Lawrence Wright, "The Man behind Bin Laden," *New Yorker,* September 16, 2002.

[107] Melissa Eddy, "German Prosecutor Says Sept. 11 Hijacker Boasted Attack Would Kill Thousands," Associated Press, August 29, 2002.

[108] Desmond Butler, "Threats and Responses: German Court; First Conviction in 9/11 Attacks," *New York Times,* February 20, 2003.

[109] Wright, "The Man behind Bin Laden."

[110] Alan Bullock, *Hitler: A Study in Tyranny* (New York, 1962), p. 408.

[111] Al-Zawahiri, *Knights under the Prophet's Banner.*

PART THREE: Europe Reverts

[1] Steven Erlanger, "Traces of Terror: The Investigation," *New York Times,* September 7, 2002.

[2] Mark Lander, "Traces of Terror: Berlin," *New York Times,* September 5, 2002.

[3] Edmund Andrews, "A Nation Challenged: Frankfurt," *New York Times,* April 24, 2002.

[4] Roger Boyes, "Terror Suspect Removed after Anti-Jew Outburst," *Times* (London), April 17, 2002.

[5] Michel Gurfinkiel, "France's Jewish Problem," *Commentary,* July/August 2002.

[6] Christopher Caldwell, "Allah Mode," *Weekly Standard,* July 15, 2002.

[7] Andreas Goldberg, "Islam in Germany," in *Islam, Europe's Second Religion: The New Social, Cultural, and Political Landscape,* ed. Shireen T. Hunter (New York, 2002), pp. 35–37.

8   John Rex, "Islam in the United Kingdom," in *Islam, Europe's Second Religion,* pp. 556–57.

9   Nezar AlSayyad, "Muslim Europe or Euro-Islam: On the Discourses of Identity and Culture," in *Muslim Europe or Euro-Islam: Politics, Culture, and Citizenship in the Age of Globalization,* ed. Nezar AlSayyad and Manuel Castells (Lanham, MD, 2002), pp. 9–29.

10 "Billions Spent by Royal Family to Spread Islam to Every Corner of the Earth," in *Ain al-Yaqeen,* March 1, 2002, in MEMRI Special Dispatch Series no. 360, March 27, 2002.

11 John Esposito, "The Muslim Diaspora and the Islamic World," in *Islam, Europe's Second Religion,* p. 248.

12 Matthew Levitt, *Targeting Terror: U.S. Policy toward Middle Eastern State Sponsors and Terrorist Organizations, Post–September 11* (Washington, 2002), p. 39.

13 *Express* (London), September 12, 2002.

14 Khalid Duran, "Jihadism in Europe," *Journal of Counterterrorism and Security International,* July 2002.

15 David Crawford and Ian Johnson, "German Muslim's Radical Path Was Paved by Saudis," *Wall Street Journal,* February 24, 2003.

16 Denis Campbell, "Shadowy World of a Sect," *Scotland on Sunday,* November 12, 1995.

17 Barry Hugill, "Muslims Pray for Delivery from Sect," *Observer* (London), March 31, 1996.

18 Pamela Sampson, "Three More Synagogues Attacked in France," Associated Press, October 14, 2000.

19 *Anti-Semitism Worldwide, 2001/2,* compiled by the Stephen Roth Institute for the Study of Contemporary Anti-Semitism and Racism at Tel Aviv University (Tel Aviv, 2001), p. 9.

20 Tim Vickery, "Rabbi Describes Attack on Kiev's Central Synagogue as a 'Pogrom,'" *Independent* (London), April 15, 2002.

21 "Four Jewish Graves Desecrated in Greek Town," Agence France-Presse, April 16, 2002.

22 "Jewish Cemetery Desecrated," Czech News Agency, April 21, 2002.

23 "Anti-Jewish Slogan Sprayed on Jewish Synagogue," Associated Press Worldstream, April 17, 2002.

24 David Smith, "Attacks on Jews Soar in Briain," *Express* (London), April 17, 2002.

25 Simcha Epstein, director of the Vidal Sassoon International Center for the Study of Anti-Semitism at the Hebrew University in Jerusalem, speaking at a symposium on "Anti-Semitism and Anti-Zionism in Western Europe since 2000"; in Elli Wohlgelernter, "France Expected to Face More Intense Wave of Anti-Semitism," *Jerusalem Post,* December 19, 2002.

26 Marlise Simons, "The Mideast in Marseille: Violence Shakes a City," *New York Times,* April 8, 2002.

27 "Nearly 360 Anti-Jewish Attacks in France in April," Associated Press, April 17, 2002.

28 Suzanne Daily, "Gang Attacks Jews on Sports Field in France," *New York Times,* April 13, 2002.

29 "Nearly 360 Anti-Jewish Attacks in France in April."

30 "Are the French Really Anti-Semitic?" *Le Monde Diplomatique,* December 2002.

31 Maria Sliwa, "The French Disconnection," *Jewsweek* (online edition), May 27, 2003, available at www.jewsweek.com.

32 "About 1,500 Residents of Bosnian Town Hold Rally in Support of Palestinians," Beta News Agency, April 12, 2002; translated by BBC Worldwide Monitoring, April 12, 2002.

33 "Sanctions and Boycott of Israeli Goods Urged at Dublin Protest," *Irish Times,* April 8, 2002.

34 "Thousands Protest in France in Support of Palestinians," Agence France-Presse, April 6, 2002.

35 "Protesters Stage pro-Palestinian Rally in Northern Greece," Associated Press Worldstream, April 15, 2002.

36 Desmond Butler, "Thousands March in Germany to Oppose Israeli Incursions," *New York Times,* April 14, 2002.

37 Christopher Caldwell, "Anti-Semitism, Anti-Americanism, Anti-Democracy," speech delivered at the YIVO Interna-

tional Conference on the Rise of Western Anti-Semitism, May 11, 2003.

38 Aleksandr Prokhanov, *Mr. Hexagen;* in Sophia Kishkovsky, "Russian Novelist Scoffs at Post-Soviet Leaders," *New York Times,* August 25, 2002.

39 *Anti-Semitism Worldwide, 2000/1,* p. 192.

40 Eszter Szamado, "Hungary to Act against Hate Speech, Racial Incitement," Agence France-Presse, October 10, 2002.

41 "Apology for Massacre; In WWII, Jews Slain by Neighbors," *Newsday,* July 11, 2001.

42 Vladimir Isachenkov, "Russian President Honors Woman Injured by Anti-Semitic Bomb," Associated Press, July 26, 2002.

43 "Backgrounder: Jean-Marie Le Pen and the National Front," Anti-Defamation League, April 23, 2002, available online at www.adl.org.

44 Ibid.

45 "Joerg Haider: The Rise of a Right-Wing Extremist," Anti-Defamation League, December 11, 1995.

46 Roger Cohen, "A Haider in Their Future," *New York Times,* April 30, 2000.

47 Gier Moulson, "German Liberals Part Company with New Member Accused of Anti-Semitic Views," Associated Press Worldstream, May 22, 2002.

48 Murray Gordon, "The New Anti-Semitism in Western Europe," American Jewish Committee, October 21, 2003, p. 5, available online at www.ajc.org.

49 "German Free Democrats Reject Anti-Semitism Charge," *Jerusalem Post,* May 19, 2002.

50 "German Liberal Leader Scolds Deputy in Anti-Semitism Row," Agence France-Presse, September 19, 2002.

51 "Synod Adopts Statement on the Relation between Christians and Jews," Lutheran World Information Service, December 7, 1998.

52 *Nostra Aetate: Declaration on the Relation of the Church to Non-Christian Religions,* proclaimed by Pope Paul VI,

October 28, 1965, available online at the Vatican website, www.vatican.va.

53 Joshua Brilliant, "Pope Pays Homage to Nazi Victims," United Press International, March 23, 2000.

54 *We Remember: A Reflection on the Shoah,* issued by the Vatican Commission for Religious Relations with Jews, March 12, 1998.

55 "Open the Archives," *Washington Post,* April 14, 2001.

56 Melanie Phillips, "Christians Who Hate the Jews," *Spectator* (London), February 16, 2002.

57 "The Return of an Ancient Hatred," *New York Times,* April 20, 2002.

58 Sam Kiley, "Sharon Vows to 'Complete' Attack on Palestinians," *Evening Standard* (London), April 8, 2002.

59 *L'Osservatore Romano,* April 2, 2002; translated by BBC Worldwide Monitoring, April 2, 2002.

60 Kayhan Website, Tehran, September 8, 2002; translated by BBC Worldwide Monitoring, September 8, 2002.

61 Randa Ghazy, *Dreaming of Palestine* (2002); translated and quoted in a public e-mail by Tom Gross, November 27, 2002.

62 Emmanuel Davidenkoff on his French National Radio show, *France Info;* translated and quoted by Tom Gross, November 27, 2002.

63 Toby Sterling, "Jewish Groups Call for ECB Chief Wim Duisenberg to Reject Wife's Statements or Resign," Associated Press Worldstream, January 10, 2003.

64 Doug Mellgren, "Nobel Committee Members Criticize Peace Laureate Peres," Associated Press, April 5, 2002.

65 Robert Mendick, "Outrage over Claire Rayner's Attack on Israel," *Independent* (London), April 21, 2002.

66 Tim Smith, "Arts Review: The Sound and the Fury," *Observer* (London), January 20, 2002.

67 Eddie Smith, "Placing Verbal Bombs," *Irish Times,* April 20, 2002.

68 A. N. Wilson, Letter to the Editor, *Daily Telegraph* (London), April 17, 2002.

69 Sam Kiley, "I Witness the Total Devastation of Sharon's 'Brutal Conquest,'" *Evening Standard* (London), April 15, 2002.

70 A. N. Wilson, "A Demo We Can't Afford to Ignore," *Evening Standard* (London), April 15, 2002.

71 "The Battle for the Truth: What Really Happened in Jenin Camp?" *Guardian* (London), April 17, 2002.

72 Janine di Giovanni, "Inside the Camp of the Dead," *Times* (London), April 16, 2002.

73 "After the Assault," *Economist,* April 27, 2002.

74 Rick Hollander, "BBC's Profiles Obscure Reality," CAMERA Report, February 5, 2003, available online at www.camera.org.

75 "More Pressure for Mid East Peace," *Guardian* (London), April 6, 2002.

76 Julie Henry, "Outrage as Oxford Bars Student for Being Israeli," *Sunday Telegraph* (London), July 29, 2003.

77 Siva Vaihyanathan, "Fired for Being Israeli," *Salon,* June 26, 2002.

78 Henrik Bachner, "Anti-Jewish Motifs in the Public Debate on Israel, Sweden: A Case Study," in *Anti-Semitism Worldwide 2001/2* (Tel Aviv, 2002).

79 *Skövde Nyheter,* June 15, 1982; in Bachner, "Anti-Jewish Motifs in the Public Debate on Israel."

80 E. van Gelium, *Dala-Demokraten,* September 22, 1982; in Bachner, "Anti-Jewish Motifs in the Public Debate on Israel."

81 *Västgöta-Demokraten,* September 21, 1982; in Bachner, "Anti-Jewish Motifs in the Public Debate on Israel."

82 William Safire, "The German Problem," *New York Times,* September 19, 2002.

83 Michael Lind, "The Weird Men behind George W. Bush's War," *New Statesman,* April 7, 2003.

84 Colin Brown and Chris Hastings, "Fury as Dalyell Attacks Blair's 'Jewish Cabal,'" *Sunday Telegraph* (London), May 4, 2003.

85 Petronella Wyatt, "Poisonous Prejudice," *Spectator* (London), December 8, 2001.

86 Barbara Amiel, "Islamists Overplay Their Hand but London Salons Don't See It," *Daily Telegraph* (London), December 17, 2001.

87 Ibid.

88 Michel Gurfinkiel, "France's Jewish Problem," *Commentary*, July/August 2002.

89 Ibid.

90 Olaf Palme, speech at the TCO-congress, July 1, 1982, published in *Dagbladet Nya Samhället*, July 9, 1982; in Bachner, "Anti-Jewish Motifs in the Public Debate on Israel."

91 Simon-Pierre Nothomb, "L'ordre va-t-il régner à Gaza?" *Le Soir*, December 18, 2001; in Joel Kotek, "Antisemitic Motifs in Belgian Anti-Israel Propaganda," in *Anti-Semitism Worldwide, 2001/2*.

92 Oona King, "Israel Can Halt This Now," *Guardian* (London), June 12, 2003.

93 Heribert Prantl, *Süddeutsche Zeitung*, April 14, 2002; in "In Europe, All-Too-Familiar Territory," *Washington Post*, April 21, 2002.

94 Ibid.

95 Jose Saramago, *El Pais*, April 21, 2001; in Paul Berman, "Bigotry in Print. Crowds Chant Murder. Something's Changed," *Forward*, May 24, 2002.

PART FOUR: The End of the American Exception?

1 Léon Poliakov, *The History of Anti-Semitism*, trans. George Klim (New York, 1985), vol. 4, p. 247.

2 Ibid., p. 252.

3 Charles M. Sennott, "Brooklyn Feels Pain of Middle East," *Boston Globe*, March 7, 1994.

4 Matthew Purdy, "Empire State Gunman's Note: Kill Zionists," *New York Times*, February 26, 1997.

5 Mike Meyers, "Violence Directed at Jews Prompts Berkeley Mayor to Propose Hate Crimes Unit," *Daily Californian*, April 26, 2002.

6 Blaine Harden, "Saudis Seek to Add U.S. Muslims to Their Sect," *New York Times,* October 20, 2001.

7 Valerie Strauss and Emily Wax, "Where Two Worlds Collide; Muslim Schools Face Tension of Islamic, U.S. Views," *Washington Post,* February 25, 2002.

8 Ibid..

9 Larry Cohler-Esses, "Sowing the Seeds of Hatred," *New York Daily News,* March 30, 2003.

10 Ibid.

11 Steven Emerson, *American Jihad: The Terrorists Living Among Us* (New York, 2002), p. 96.

12 Mark Goldwert, "Excerpt from 'Protocols' Appears in Patterson Paper," *New Jersey Jewish News,* November 7, 2002.

13 Michelle Goldberg, "My Arab Street," *Salon.com,* March 7, 2003.

14 Harden, "Saudis Seek to Add U.S. Muslims to Their Sect."

15 *ADL Special Report: Louis Farrakhan in His Own Words,* Anti-Defamation League (1994), p. 3.

16 E. R. Shipp, "Chicago Muslim Gets Qaddafi Loan," *New York Times,* May 4, 1985.

17 "Farrakhan in Iraq for 'Solidarity' Visit," United Press International, July 6, 2002.

18 Dirk Johnson, "Farrakhan Ends Longtime Rivalry with Orthodox Muslims," *New York Times,* February 28, 2000.

19 Paul M. Barrett, "Saudi Influence in the US: How a Muslim Chaplain Spread Extremism to an Inmate Flock," *Wall Street Journal,* February 5, 2003.

20 Ibid.

21 *Audit of Anti-Semitic Incidents,* Anti-Defamation League (2001), p. 18.

22 David Talbot, "Buchanan's Pen Stirs National Furor," *Boston Herald,* February 25, 1996.

23 Jude Wanniski, "Do Jews Control the Media?" memo to Mortimer B. Zuckerman, available online at www.wanniski.com.

24 Earl Raab, "The Black Revolution and the Jewish Question," *Commentary,* January 1969.

25 Khalid Abdul Mohammed, "Who Is It Sucking Our Blood?" in "Jackson Joined," *Newsday,* January 24, 1994.

26 Steve Miller and Amy Fagan, "Linder Beats Barr in Georgia Primary; McKinney Also Loses Re-election Bid," *Washington Times,* August 21, 2002.

27 John Mercurio, "Racially Charged; Middle East Politics Heat up Alabama House Contest," *Roll Call,* May 2, 2002.

28 William Saletan and Avi Zenilman, "The Gaffes of Al Sharpton," *Slate.com,* October 7, 2003.

29 Jeff Jacoby, "The Fires of Hatred in the Age of Farrakhan," *Boston Globe,* December 14, 1995.

30 Maria Newman, "Poet Laureate Stands by Words against Israel and Won't Step Down," *New York Times,* October 3, 2002.

31 Ibid.

32 Stanley Crouch, "Poet Laureate Was a Bad Hire," *New York Daily News,* October 3, 2002.

33 Walter Fields, "Baraka Asks Legitimate Questions," *New Jersey Rrecord,* October 8, 2002.

34 Wilbert A. Tatum, "Somebody Did Blow up America," *Amsterdam News* (New York), October 9, 2002.

35 "New Jersey's Poet Dilemma," *New York Times,* editorial, October 4, 2002.

36 "Featuring Diverse Views Promotes Free Speech," *Stanford Daily,* October 22, 2002.

37 Jonathan Mark, "Poets against the Jews: Academic Freedom Gets Tested at Harvard and Yeshiva," *Jewish Week,* February 21, 2003.

38 Ibid.

39 Marcella Fleming, "IU Hillel: Pig Head Account Untrue; Director Discounts Story Columnist Used as Example of Campus Anti-Semitism in U.S.," *Indianapolis Star,* October 11, 2002.

40 Andrea Peyser, "Rutgers Gets 'F' for Putting Anti-Semitism 101 on the Schedule," *New York Post,* July 9, 2003.

41 Tunku Varadarajan, "Revolting at Rutgers," *Wall Street Journal,* April 19, 2002.

42 Aleza Goldsmith, "Bigotry by the Bay," *Jerusalem Post,* June 7, 2002.

43 Georgetown University Professor Halim Barakat, "The Wild Beast That Zionism Created: Self-Destruction," *Al-Hayat* (London), April 4, 2002; translated by MEMRI, cited in Special Dispatch Series no. 369, April 16, 2002.

44 Elli Wohlgelernter, "Take Back the University," *Jerusalem Post,* August 9, 2002.

45 Karen Alexander, "West Bank; San Francisco Dispatch," *New Republic,* June 24, 2002.

46 Millie Lapidario and Wendy Lee, "Pro-Palestinian Class Proposal under Review at UC-Berkeley," *Daily Californian,* May 10, 2002.

47 Melissa Radler, "Anti-Semitic Riot at San Francisco State University," *Jerusalem Post,* May 16, 2002.

48 Goldsmith, "Bigotry by the Bay."

49 Alexander, "West Bank; San Francisco Dispatch."

50 Jenna Russell, "Some on Harvard, MIT Faculties Urge Divestment in Israel," *Boston Globe,* May 6, 2002.

51 Tom Tugend, "California Governor Calls for Crackdown on Anti-Semitism at State Universities," Jewish Telegraphic Agency, July 23, 2002.

52 Fred M. Donner, "OK, President Bush, What If...?" *Chicago Tribune,* March 10, 2003.

53 Stanley Hoffmann, "The High and the Mighty," *American Prospect,* January 13, 2003.

54 Georgie Anne Geyer, "Mideast Campaigns Could Isolate America," *Chicago Tribune,* October 26, 2001.

55 Joel Kovel, "Anti-Semitism on the Left and the Special Status of Israel," *Tikkun,* May 2003.

56 Paul Buhle, "The Civil Liberties Crisis and the Threat of 'Too Much Democracy,'" *Tikkun,* May 2003.

57 Jason A. Vest, "The Men from JINSA and CSP," *Nation,* September 2, 2002.

58 Kathleen and Bill Christison, "A Rose by Any Other Name: The Bush Administration's Dual Loyalties," *Washington Report on Middle East Affairs,* March, 2003.

59 Edward Said, "A Monument to Hypocrisy," *Al-Ahram,* February 13–19, 2003.

60 Zev Chafets, "Prof's Slip Is Showing—So's His Anti-Semitism," *New York Daily News,* February 19, 2003.

61 Bret Stephens, "The Zionist Cabal," *Jerusalem Post,* March 21, 2003.

62 Michael Lind, "The Israel Lobby" and "Israel Lobby Part 3," *Prospect,* March 21, 2002 and September 26, 2002.

63 Lind, "Israel Lobby Part 3."

64 Lind, "The Israel Lobby."

65 Léon Poliakov, *The History of Anti-Semitism,* trans. George Klim (New York, 1985), vol. 4, p. 231.

66 Ibid., p. 234.

67 Patrick J. Buchanan, "Whose War?" *American Conservative,* March 24, 2003.

68 Patrick J. Buchanan, "Is the Neoconservative Movement Over?" *American Conservative,* June 16, 2003.

69 Buchanan, "Whose War?"

70 Richard Curtis, "Wolfowitz and His Successfully Evil Cabal," *Arab News,* February 23, 2003.

71 Bob Dart and William Wan, "Diverse Protesters Fill D.C.; Thousands Back Palestinian Cause," *Atlanta Journal and Constitution,* April 21, 2002.

72 "The Note," *ABC News,* February 12, 2002; in *Hotline,* February 12, 2003.

73 In *Hotline,* March 10, 2003.

74 Poliakov, *The History of Anti-Semitism,* vol. 1, p. 69n.

75 Larissa MacFarquhar, "The Devil's Accountant," *New Yorker,* March 31, 2003.

76 "Noam Chomsky on Israel, the US and Palestine," interview with the *Socialist Worker,* March 24, 2001.

77 Norman G. Finkelstein, "First the Carrot, Then the Stick: Behind the Carnage in Palestine," April 14, 2002, available online at www.normanfinkelstein.com.

78 Zeina Karam, "U.S. Author Likens Israeli Actions to Nazi Persecution," Associated Press Worldstream, December 10, 2001.

79 Norman G. Finkelstein, *The Holocaust Industry: Reflections on the Exploitation of Jewish Suffering* (New York, 2000), pp. 35, 37.

80 "Anti-Semitism on the Left and the Special Status of Israel," *Tikkun,* May 1, 2003.

81 "We Renounce Israel Rights," Letter to the Editor, *Guardian* (London), August 8, 2002.

82 Uri Avnery, "Manufacturing Anti-Semites," *Tikkun,* November 2002. This piece also appeared in *Arab-American News,* December 6, 2002.

83 Israel Shahak, *Jewish History, Jewish Religion: The Weight of Three Thousand Years* (London, 1994), Chapter 6.

84 Alan Dershowitz, "Noam Chomsky's Immoral Petition," *Jerusalem Post,* May 16, 2002.

85 MacFarquhar, "The Devil's Accountant."

86 Kyra Phillips interview with Adam Shapiro, CNN *Sunday Morning,* March 31, 2002.

87 P. C. Shivadas, "Correcting Distorted History," *New Straits Times* (Malaysia), April 13, 2002.

88 Amir Mizroch, "Malaysian Officials Hand out Copy of 'International Jew,'" *Jerusalem Post,* June 22, 2003.

89 Roziana Hamsawi, "Foreign Media Reports on Palestinian Issue Unfair, Says Activist," *New Straits Times* (Malaysia), June 16, 2003.

90 *New York Times,* March 22, 2002.

91 Michael Lerner, "Tikkun Mail," July 14, 2002.

92 Paul McCloskey, chairman of the Council for the National Interest, speaking at the Tikkun Community Conference and Teach-In to Congress, June 2, 2003.

93 Mark H. Ellis, "On the Jewish Civil War and the New Prophetic," *Tikkun,* July 2001.

94 Mark H. Ellis, *Practicing Exile: The Religious Odyssey of an American Jew* (Minneapolis, 2002), pp. 160–61.

95 Emma Schwartz and Jay Kapp, "Former Israeli Prime Minister Speaks on UC-Berkeley Campus," *Daily Californian,* November 20, 2002.

96 Susannah Heschel, "Whither the Zionist Dream?" *Tikkun,* May 2003.

97 International Solidarity Movement "Call Out for Mature ISMers and Jewish ISMers," at www.palestinemonitor.org, May 22, 2003.

98 Patrick J. Buchanan, "Whose War?" *American Conservative,* March 24, 2003.

99 Tavis Smiley interview with Cornel West, National Public Radio, June 26, 2003.

100 Paul Cullen, "'I Won't Lie Down and Take the Insults,'" *Irish Times,* July 1, 2003.

101 Mohamed Sid-Ahmed, "Noam Chomsky in Cairo: Chomsky's Duality," *Al-Ahram,* May 20, 1993.

102 Tutu and Said quotations are from the cover page of Marc Ellis's *Revolutionary Forgiveness: Essays on Judaism, Christianity, and the Future of Religious Life* (Texas, 2000).

103 Christopher Hitchens, "Israel Shahak, 1933–2001," *Nation,* July 23, 2001.

PART FIVE: Descent into Delusion

1 Maggie Michael, "Mubarak's Top Adviser Urges Egyptian, Arab Writers to Curb Anti-Semitic Opinions," Associated Press, December 30, 2002.

2 Pascal Boniface, "Letter to an Israeli Friend," *Le Monde,* August 2001; quoted in Christopher Caldwell, "Liberté, Egalité, Judeophobie," *Weekly Standard,* May 6, 2002.

3 Tim Vickery, "Youths Attack Ukrainian Synagogue with Stones and Bottles," Associated Press Worldstream, April 14, 2002.

4 Caldwell, "Liberté, Egalité, Judeophobie."

5 Oriana Fallaci, "On Jew-Hatred in Europe," *Corriere della sera,* April 2002; unofficial translation by David Harris, American Jewish Committee, www.ajc.org.

6 Tavis Smiley interview with Louis Farrakhan, National Public Radio, June 26, 2003.

7 Patrick J. Buchanan, "Whose War?" *American Conservative,* March 24, 2003.

8   Amitai Etzioni, "Harsh Lessons in Incivility," *Chronicle of Higher Education,* November 1, 2002.
9   Joel Kovel, "Zionism's Bad Conscience," *Tikkun,* September 2002.
10 Slobodan Lekic, "Malaysian Leader Refuses to Back Down on Remarks about Jews at Islamic Summit," Associated Press, October 17, 2003.
11 Emil Fackenheim, Letter to the Editor, *Commentary,* October 2002.
12 Etzioni, "Harsh Lessons in Incivility."
13 "An Ugly Rumor or an Ugly Truth?" *New York Times,* August 4, 2002.
14 Arch Puddington, "The Wages of Durban," *Commentary,* November, 2001.
15 Ibid.
16 Hillel Halkin, "The Return of Anti-Semitism," *Commentary,* February 2002.
17 Léon Poliakov, *The History of Anti-Semitism,* trans. George Klim (New York, 1985), vol. 3, p. 376.
18 Ibid., p. 376.
19 Puddington, "The Wages of Durban."
20 Chris Tomlinson, "Forum on Side of Human Rights Conference Condemns Israel," Associated Press, September 2, 2001.
21 Leon Wieseltier, "Hitler Is Dead: Against Ethnic Panic," *New Republic,* May 27, 2002.
22 Ibid.
23 Tony Judt, "Israel: The Alternative," *New York Review of Books,* October 23, 2003.
24 Tony Judt, "The Way We Live Now," *New York Review of Books,* March 27, 2003.
25 Ibid.
26 Tony Judt, "The Road to Nowhere," *New York Review of Books,* May 9, 2002; and Judt, "Israel: The Alternative."
27 Judt, "Israel: The Alternative."
28 George Jonas, "Evil Intentions: Nasty Weapons of Iran,

Iraq, North Korea More Worrisome Than Those of Britain, France," *Gazette* (Montreal), February 24, 2002.

29 Wieseltier, "Hitler Is Dead: Against Ethnic Panic."

30 "Former Iran President Says Mideast Nuclear Conflict Possible," Agence France-Presse, December 14, 2001.

31 "Pronouncements by Muslim Religious Leaders Defending Suicide Attacks," compiled by the Israel Foreign Ministry, September 1997; available online at www.israel-mfa.gov.il.

32 Joel Brinkley, "Arabs' Grief in Bethlehem, Bombers' Gloating in Gaza," *New York Times,* April 4, 2002.

33 Richard John Neuhaus, "Israel and Anti-Semitism," in "The Public Square: A Continuing Survey of Religion and Public Life," *First Things,* May 2002.

34 Paul Craig Roberts, "Fight World War IV—Or Let Israelis Immigrate?" September 24, 2002, www.vdare.com.

35 Norman Cohn, *Warrant for Genocide* (New York, 1966), p. 268.

INDEX

181